A Radical In The East

Second Edition Revised

A Radical In The East

Second Edition Revised

S. Brent Morris, PhD

Past Master, Patmos-Solomon's Lodge No. 70,
Savage, Maryland

Past Master, Quatuor Coronati Lodge No. 2076,
London

Fellow of the Philalethes Society

Past Grand Abbot, Society of Blue Friars

Westphalia Press
An Imprint of the Policy Studies Organization
Washington, DC
2022

A Radical In The East: Second Edition Revised
All Rights Reserved © 2022 by Policy Studies Organization

Westphalia Press
An imprint of Policy Studies Organization
1527 New Hampshire Ave., NW
Washington, D.C. 20036
info@ipsonet.org

ISBN: 978-1-63723-914-8

Cover and interior design by Jeffrey Barnes
jbarnesbook.design

Daniel Gutierrez-Sandoval, Executive Director
PSO and Westphalia Press

Updated material and comments on this edition
can be found at the Westphalia Press website:
www.westphaliapress.org

To the memory of

Jerry E. Marsengill

PM, FPS, 32°, KCCH, PGHP, PGM, MBMC

Friend · Mentor · Editor · Master Mason

Contents

(Cont'd.)

Foreword to the Second Edition

In 1993 I was thrust into the task of assisting S. Brent Morris in the first edition of *A Radical In The East*. Sixteen years later I have been asked to write a new foreword to this remarkable book, moving from the back to the front of the volume! In order to accomplish this, I took the opportunity to reread this book and I found it just as timely for today's Mason as it was then. Brother Morris speaks truths that are timeless.

A Radical in the East was and is a forward-looking book. It does not dwell on the past except to analyze the conditions that have led us to the fraternity of today. Brother S. Brent Morris is a mathematician and he looks at the problems of Masonry with a mathematician's eye. He is also a Mason with a long experience with Craft, York, and Scottish Rite Masonry. There are few, if any, Masons who can claim the experience that Brother Morris has. Since the book originally came out, he has continued his Masonic accomplishments. He was awarded the Grand Cross of the Court of Honour in the Ancient and Accepted Scottish Rite of Freemasonry, Southern Jurisdiction, in 1999. Most recently, he has just completed a term as Master of Quatuor Coronati Lodge No. 2076, London, the premier research lodge in the world. A complete list of his accomplishments would fill more space that I have been allotted for this forward.

Brother Morris' books have cleared the cobwebs from Freemasonry. He has appeared on national radio and television and has brought reasonable answers to questions that have been asked about our fraternity. His work has brought a new level of scholarship to Freemasonry. He does not write something unless he has researched it and tested it and when he does say something it is worth listening to—more than once.

Brother Morris has added two additional papers to the book. "Voting with their Feet" and an article about Scottish Rite membership are worthy additions to the collection and add to the overall theme of the book. Keith Arrington left it up to the reader in the original forward to decide whether or not Brother Morris was a radical. This book has shaped my thinking about Freemasonry and the need for the Craft to address the problems that (still) face it today. I think that Brother Morris would agree with me that leadership needs to lead and not just "hold a place" for a year. *A Radical In The*

East is a guidebook to action by Masons or groups of Masons who are interested in learning about our Craft and its membership problems and ways to address them. It can be read and studied by individuals, study groups or even entire lodges. There is a lot of value in this little book. There is much food for thought and discussion. I recommend it to any serious student of Masonry.

JAY COLE SIMSER, PGHP

Foreword to the First Edition

A self-professed "Radical in the East," Brent Morris is a Masonic scholar, author, lecturer, and book reviewer and is Executive Secretary of the Editorial Board of *The Scottish Rite Journal*. He has served in the Masonic East and lives and works on the East Coast, in the United States Capitol area.

Although an Easterner by residence (he was born in Texas), Brent has an Iowa-Midwest connection in that he was, in a sense, the Masonic protégé of the late Franklin J. "Andy" Anderson, Iowa school teacher, Assistant Librarian of the Iowa Masonic Library and, later, assistant to the editor of *The Royal Arch Mason*. Andy retired to Columbia, Maryland, where he served as Executive Secretary of the Philalethes Society. When he relinquished that office, the Philalethes secretary's pen was turned over to his young friend, S. Brent Morris, who filled the office with distinction for several years.

The recipient of many Masonic honors, Brent Morris is a Fellow of the Philalethes Society and wears the white cap of the 33° of the Scottish Rite.

This collection of papers, which have been presented by Brother Morris in such far-flung Masonic scenes as Minnesota and Texas, as well as on the East Coast, presents something of interest, information, and a challenge for everyone. Whether or not the brother is a radical will be decided by you, the reader. In any case, you will be impressed with his scholarship and caught up by his enthusiasm.

Brother Morris examines, as a professional mathematician and statistician, the persistent problems of shrinking Masonic membership and nonattendance at meetings with fresh viewpoints and a realistic but optimistic outlook. He also provides a wealth of informative and relaxing reading about Masonry for those who never tire of learning more about our fraternity. As an amateur magician, it is possible that Brent may have insight that is denied to other mere mortals.

A Radical In The East was the last book chosen by Jerry Marsengill, founder, editor, and moving force behind Iowa Research Lodge No. 2, for publication by that body.

KEITH ARRINGTON, FPS, BF
Grand Librarian Emeritus, Iowa

Preface to the Second Edition

If you want to make God smile, announce your plans.

If I thought it was exciting sixteen years ago to be invited to assemble a collection of my papers on Freemasonry, then it's doubly so to be asked to prepare a second edition. It is humbling to think that someone is still interested in reading essays written as much as twenty-seven years ago!

The oldest essay here, "A Radical in the East," still conveys my frustration after finishing a year as High Priest of a Royal Arch Chapter, but I'm not sure that my "radical" proposals—serving liquor, abandoning top hats and formal wear, simplifying ceremonies, and holding more interesting meetings—are all that important now, except for holding more interesting meetings. (Who could disagree with that!) The York Rite has continued its decline to the point that in many places it's lost its "critical mass," that is, enough members for it to function. For example, a few years ago the Cryptic Masons of Maryland could not find anyone willing to start in the bottom of the line to the Grand East.

I think the second oldest essay, "Trends Affecting American Freemasonry," has held up better, as have most of my statistical and historical papers. My discovery that many fraternal groups peaked in membership before the Depression calls into question our understanding of how Freemasonry and other fraternal groups fit in to American Society, and the puzzle of the ascendancy of the Scottish Rite over the York Rite in twentieth-century America still remains. Prof. Robert Putnam's 2000 book, *Bowling Alone,* was a nice confirmation that declining Masonic memberships are part of a larger societal trend. (We're still drowning, but largely for reasons that appear to be beyond our control.)

Perhaps the main thing that I have learned since writing these essays is that changing membership trends is like turning an aircraft carrier. There are no simple answers and no quick fixes, only persistent hard work. One of the reasons that change is so difficult in Freemasonry and other voluntary associations is that our members (including me!) who have stuck with the fraternity and have become its leaders pretty much like it the way it is. Significant change, which is probably necessary, is outside of our comfort zone and might lead to an organization different from the one we love.

When I assembled the first edition of *A Radical in the East,* I was a mathematician working for the federal government. One of the things that attracted me to majoring in mathematics was that I didn't have to produce term papers or other written material on a deadline. In 2000, I retired from the government and went to work for the Supreme Council, 33°, S.J., in the newly created position of Director of Membership Development. It was an opportunity to put some of my theories into practice. In 2005 I became editor of *The Scottish Rite Journal* and now regularly produce written material on a deadline. I'm having fun, and I'm sure that God is smiling!

It will be interesting to see if in another twenty-seven years anyone wants a third edition.

S. Brent Morris, pm, fps, bf
Laurel, Maryland, June 12, 2009

Preface to the First Edition

I t was exciting to have my good friend and the noted Masonic scholar, Jerry Marsengill, agree to publish a collection of my papers for Iowa Research Lodge No. 2. My enthusiasm has been tempered, however, by his untimely passing; my self-confidence has been tested by carefully rereading these early literary efforts.

It is all too easy for authors to think of their writings as timeless gems of wisdom, to be sought eagerly by future generations. Some of my writing has aged quite well, I think, but time has not been so kind to all. Why did I use such a trite phrase there? Did I really think those words were so clever (when they sound so clichéd now)?

My first temptation was to rewrite every paper. In some cases, I have additional facts and better references. In others, I could make my point in fewer and stronger words. If nothing else, I could use a consistent style for references. With a great deal of effort, I resisted these noble urges.

There should be some value in seeing an author's ideas evolve and his style mature. If nothing else, the passion that inspired me to write some papers might be lost by careful polishing and refining. You have here what I published—not what I should have written.

Indications of radicalism appeared early in my Masonic career: I've always asked questions. "On Masonic Research" reveals some of the first questions I raised about our gentle craft, even before I was initiated. When I was appointed to the officer's line in Patmos Lodge, I did the unthinkable: I read the Constitution of the Grand Lodge of Maryland. After that I was always asking, "Where does it say that in the Constitution?" Later I posed other questions: "If it's such a great idea, why didn't it work for the Odd Fellows?" Like Jerry Marsengill, I discovered that some Masonic "leaders" don't like questions (especially carefully researched and documented ones).

I don't expect you to agree with everything I've written, but I do hope you will think about the issues I raise. I had fun writing these papers, and I hope you will enjoy reading them.

S. BRENT MORRIS, PM, FPS
Columbia, Maryland, July 26, 1993

Trends Affecting
American Freemasonry

A Commentary on Declines in Fraternalism in General and in the York Rite in Particular

The winds and the waves are always on the side of the ablest navigators.

—Edward Gibbon

Anyone considering the current condition of Freemasonry in general, and of the York and Scottish Rites in particular, should be aware of two overriding trends. First, and externally, fraternal membership is not now the social norm in the United States. Second, and internally, the Scottish Rite is steadily supplanting the York Rite as the avenue of additional light and activity for American Freemasons. These trends are not malevolent conspiracies with some sinister direction but are reflections of the society in which we live. We must attempt to understand these trends, or resign ourselves to being mindlessly buffeted by the winds and waves of social forces.

The first trend, that of declining fraternal membership in the United States, has been a fact since about 1920. At that time Charles Merz, in an article in *Harper's Magazine,* estimated there were 800 secret orders with 30 million members—and this was when the U.S. adult population was only 60 million! Most of these organizations came into existence between 1860 and 1920 and now are either dead or in a state of organizational senility. What caused that phenomenal growth and, most recently, the precipitous decline?

The organizations came into being to meet various needs of our populace. Following the Civil War, many yearned for some sense of brotherly love to reunite the country. Immigrants sought the comfort of their own countrymen, and wanted benefits such as life or burial insurance that were denied them by commercial insurance companies. Benevolence in fact was a major attraction of fraternal membership. This ranged from finding employment, nursing care, payments during illness, burial services, and care of widows and orphans—all of which were guaranteed in lodge bylaws. Finally, there was the matter of social prestige. Schmidt and Babchuk in "Trends in U.S. Fraternal Associations in the Twentieth Century" incisively state the operation of the prestige factor:

> Traditionally the United States has laid great emphasis on the value of equality, which logically does not support an emphasis on the differences   in ritual and ceremony.... It was particularly in the small town, where practically no one was a stranger, that lodge ritual and ceremony meant most. Fraternal members could impress fellow townsmen that, by belonging to certain groups, they were different and distinctive.[5]

Throughout this period, Freemasonry enjoyed a position of preeminence: it was the oldest and most widespread of American fraternities; its membership included many heroes of the American Revolution; it must have enjoyed a certain intriguing reputation from the anti-Masonic period such a short time before; and it guaranteed no benefits to its members. There were no employment promises, no guaranteed sick payments, no certain burial benefits. In contrast, Odd Fellowship, for example, guaranteed many of these benefits. Thus a Mason had enough discretionary income (and perforce social prestige) to enable him to join a group that promised so little, though the benefits usually accrued in any event. As long as fraternalism fulfilled certain needs of American society, Freemasonry, the most prestigious of fraternities, was an inadvertent beneficiary.

By the 1920s, fundamental changes in American society were beginning to cause changes in fraternities. Table 1 shows the last year of growth before the Depression for several American fraternal orders. It is important to note that nearly all had experienced declining membership before 1929, and in fact had only insignificant increases before their last year of growth.[1, 2, 6]

By this time, many of the needs formerly filled by fraternal orders either were not pressing or were met by other groups. The great waves of immigrants had stopped and, as earlier immigrants became integrated into the mainstream of American life, there was less need for exclusively ethnic fraternal groups. Insurance was now more widely available to most Americans, and the state, through various social service agencies, began to assume more and more responsibility for the welfare of citizens. Today, for example, improved health care, greater job safety, and a declining birthrate, among many other factors, have almost eliminated the need for orphanages.

1921: Knights of Pythias

1923: Odd Fellows

1925: Grotto

1926: Knights Templar

Royal Arch Masons

Shriners

Knights of Columbus

1927: Royal and Select Masters

1928: Freemasons

1929: Scottish Rite

TABLE 1. Last Year of Growth for Some American Fraternal Orders

The increasing urbanization of America and the anonymity that necessarily accompanies it also took their toll. Schmidt and Babchuk clearly captured that thought:

> the relatively high social status [fraternal] lodges once enjoyed is, of course, peculiar to a time when the United States was essentially a small-town society. Today, with increasing anonymity in the urban environment, pomp and ceremony, apparently, have become less meaningful. (After all, what does it mean to impress strangers, if, indeed, one can impress them at all?)[5]

An unadvertised benefit of fraternal membership one hundred years ago was the business contacts offered. This aspect was so popular that it led to the formation of businessmen's clubs (usually termed service organizations) such as Rotary, Kiwanis, and so on. For those interested in a specific type of service to their fellow man, there are now scores of volunteer groups, such as the Red Cross, the American Cancer Society, and others that specialize in aid and help.

Finally, as ever larger numbers of Americans joined fraternal groups of one sort or another, the social prestige these organizations once offered (as exclusive groups with limited memberships) necessarily diminished. Thus status seekers left the lodges for ever more exclusive domains, such as country clubs. This trend was noted as early as 1940 by Noel Gist in his work, *Secret Societies: A Cultural Study of Fraternalism in the United States.*[3]

In short, the secular needs once met by fraternal orders either are no longer compelling needs, or are now more efficiently met by narrower groups. The young businessman of today seeking business contacts, community recognition, and social prestige would be best advised to join Rotary, work with the Heart Fund, and seek membership in a country club. Fraternal membership is not now the social norm for young men, and this must be recognized in studying Freemasonry today.

The second major trend, that of the ascendancy of the Scottish Rite over the York Rite, is internal to Freemasonry, but is nonetheless important to understand. In 1900, the Ancient and Accepted Scottish Rite comprised a mere 4% of the Freemasons in the United States. Their Valleys were in urban centers, while the population was dispersed in small, rural communities. The governmental structure of the Scottish Rite, that of a self-perpetuating hierarchy, was distinctly at odds with the representative democracy of the York Rite. With 26% of American Masons then in chapters and 14% in commanderies, who could have guessed the current situation! Today [1982], the percentage of Master Masons in the chapter is 19%, the percentage who are Knights Templar has dropped by one fourth to 11%, and the percentage who are in the Scottish Rite has increased nearly nine-fold to 35%. This can only be described as a fundamental realignment of the Craft.

Let's consider for a moment why this shift may have occurred. To begin with, it would be pure sophistry to argue about the relative superiority of the moral teachings of the York or Scottish Rites. Rather, the proper area of comparison is that of organizational structure. Here now are a few thoughts on why the York Rite has been overwhelmed by the Scottish Rite.

From a purely marketing point of view, being a "32° Mason" sounds more important than being a Knight Templar. When the Shrine declared the Thirty-Second Degree and the Order of the Temple to be equivalent, at least for their purposes, and as the attraction of the Shrine has grown, distinctions between the Rites became blurred. For those interested primarily in Shrine membership, the Scottish Rite could provide the avenue in less time.

In the earlier part of the century, the York Rite required catechisms between degrees in some bodies, and prospective Sir Knights faced the financial burden of buying a uniform. Thus those uninterested in memorization or uniforms, together with non-Christians, had no opportunity for full participation in the York Rite. The rules and procedures of the Ancient and Accepted Rite stood in distinct contrast to this.

In the Scottish Rite, there is one supreme recognition for achievement—the Thirty-Third Degree, which can be attained through many different types of service. In contrast, the York Rite offers no honor with comparable universal recognition or prestige and virtually no rewards for any but presiding officers. For all practical purposes, a Scottish Rite Mason is active either in his Valley or not at all, while a York Rite Mason is all but urged to disperse his efforts away from his local bodies. (After serving at the local level, the York Rite Mason is encouraged to serve in the district, then in the state, and then in the national bodies, not to mention the myriad of "honor" organizations he may be invited to join.) Finally, but certainly not exhausting the list of reasons for Scottish Rite dominance, the population migration to urban centers has directly benefited the centralized and urban Scottish Rite, to the detriment of the dispersed and rural York Rite.

Now, how do these trends help us understand Freemasonry today? Because it is not the social norm to belong to a fraternal order today, we cannot really expect to attract many deeply committed Master Masons by improving public relations, by allowing solicitation, by undertaking a host of service projects, or by using any of a score of equally silly ideas. We may as well try to encourage a return to bow ties and double-breasted suits (which are now simply not the fashion norm).

The problem of declining membership is like a bucket of sand with a slowly dropping level. Simply pouring more sand into the top at an ever-faster rate doesn't solve the basic problem—sand is running out somewhere. Until the bucket is plugged, the problem is still with us.

What we should do now is to consider ways to encourage our members to full activity and to remove as many needless barriers to participation as possible. We should not be satisfied with allowing only one man per year to serve and be rewarded in each body, and then only by his skill as a parrot. We must critically examine our procedures and decide if we may actually discourage new Masons from activity. We cannot be satisfied with throwing more and more candidates into our ceremonies until we can satisfactorily explain why so many choose not to stay and participate. The alternative is to be helplessly and hopelessly at the mercy of the winds and waves of external forces. The real danger is that we may break up on the shoals of indecision and join the flotsam of other noble fraternities that have lacked the foresight of able navigators.

REFERENCES

1. Anderson, Albin C. "Summary of Candidates and Membership—1924 to 1951 Inclusive." Manuscript, New York, 1952.

2. Denslow, Ray Vaughn. *Is Anything Wrong with Templarism?* N.p. [Missouri?]: N.d. [1929?].

3. Gist, Noel. *Secret Societies: A Cultural Study of Fraternalism in the United States.* University of Missouri Studies, 1940, pp. 9–176.

4. Merz, Charles. "Sweet Land of Secrecy." *Harpers Monthly Magazine,* 154 (1927), pp. 329–34.

5. Schmidt, Alvin J. and Nicholas Babchuk. "Trends in U.S. Fraternal Associations in the Twentieth Century." *Voluntary Action Research: 1973.* David Horton, ed. Lexington Books, 1973.

6. Supreme Lodge, Knights of Pythias. "Membership Totals: 1864 to 1976."Manuscript, Stockton, Calif., n.d. (ca. 1976).

Paper presented to Maryland Masonic Research Society, February 6, 1982

Boom to Bust in the Twentieth Century

Freemasonry and American Fraternities

People got to where they didn't want to join up any more. Can you imagine that? ... little by little the lodges jest sorter dried up. Nobody wanted to join. No new people. Jesus, but we was big once ... Hell, there was governors and senators that was Brother Knights. We had conventions and barbecues and parades. Took over the whole hotel there in Tulsa. Gawd, and it musta been somethin' to see.

—L. D. to Lonnie Roy[1]
The Last Meeting of the Knights of the White Magnolia, Preston Jones

The twentieth century has been a period of unprecedented growth, expansion, and change for the United States of America. The summaries have begun to sound trite, but we indeed have moved from horses to moon shuttles within a few decades. America has moved from a rural, agrarian economy to an urban, service one. For good or bad, change has been an inescapable feature of all of American life, including Freemasonry and American fraternities. The effect of these changes on fraternal orders can be neatly (and sadly) described as boom to bust.

The plaintive summary by L. D. of what happened to the Knights of the White Magnolia could describe most fraternal orders today. The surprising fact is that at the beginning of the century, it would have been hard to predict today's fraternal conditions. In just fifteen years from 1885 to 1900, more than 150 American fraternal organizations were formed![2] If some sort of group was formed then, for almost any purpose, it likely modeled itself along fraternal lines with elaborate rituals, formal ceremonies, membership hierarchies, and colorful regalia. By 1920, Charles Merz estimated that there were 800 secret orders with a combined total of 30 million members—and this was when the adult U.S. population was only 60 million![3]

---

1   Preston Jones, *The Last Meeting of the Knights of the White Magnolia, A Texas Trilogy* (New York: Hill and Ward, 1976).

2   Alvin J. Schmidt, *Fraternal Organizations* (Westport, CT: Greenwood Press, 1980), 370–73.

3   Charles Merz, "Sweet Land of Secrecy," *Harpers' Monthly Magazine,* 154 (1927), 329.

Fraternal orders went well beyond being the normative form for community groups, and, at least for the uniformed, military orders, such as the Knights Templar or the Knights of Pythias, the groups were considered an important adjunct to the nation's defense. John T. Thompson, Second Lieutenant of the U.S. Artillery wrote on this a century ago:

> For a reserve the country depends upon the veterans of the [Civil] war, and the national guards of the states. Closely behind this force, and equally strong in numbers comes a new factor in the national defense. The hundred thousand members of the military branches of the four great secret fraternities in this country would, in an emergency, respond as citizens, by companies and battalions. ... [4]

Significant changes have occurred in American society this century, changes which seem to have effectively abandoned fraternities as a meaningful part of American culture. The dramatic changes in fortunes for these groups are matters of objective curiosity and subjective dismay. This paper will concentrate on an objective description of fraternal memberships during the last eighty or so years.

The analysis begins by studying the national membership figures for major American fraternal organizations at five-year intervals from 1900 to 2000 (see Appendix). The fraternities studied include Freemasons, the Order of the Eastern Star, the Independent Order of Odd Fellows, Rebekahs, Patriarchs, Patriarchs Militant, Knights of Pythias, Scottish Rite, the Shriners, the Elks, the Knights of Columbus, Royal Arch Masons, Royal and Select Masters, and the Knights Templar.

The statistical technique of cluster analysis was then used to produce four fraternal groupings, each consisting of organizations that had very similar membership movements during the twentieth century. By separating the organizations into similar groups, it is possible to better understand what forces are affecting fraternities in general.

The four clusters are 1) Freemasons, 2) Odd Fellows, 3) Scottish Rite, and 4) York Rite (see Table 1). The Freemason Cluster includes the Eastern Star. The Odd Fellow Cluster consists of the Odd Fellow auxiliaries the

---

4 James R. Carnahan, *Pythian Knighthood: Its History and Literature* (Cincinnati: Pettibone Mfg. Co., 1888), 455. The "the four great secret fraternities" were probably the Uniformed Rank, Knights of Pythias, Grand Army of the Republic, Patriarchs Militant of the Odd Fellows, and the Knights Templar of the York Rite of Masonry.

Patriarchs, the Patriarchs Militant, and the Rebekah, together with the Knights of Pythias. The Scottish Rite Cluster has the Shriners, the Elks, and the Knights of Columbus. The York Rite Cluster includes Royal Arch Masons, Royal and Select Masters, and the Knights Templar. A detailed description of each cluster is given below.

Table 1: U.S. Fraternal Clusters

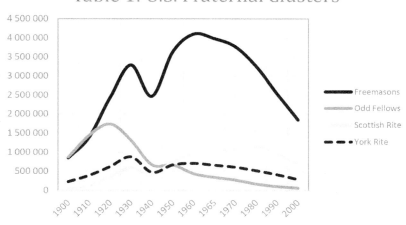

TABLE 1. US Fraternal Clusters, 1900–2000

What Happened?

Freemasons

Still the largest fraternal organization in the United States (though not under a central, national administration), Freemasonry continues to exert an influence, albeit declining, upon America. It is grouped here with the Order of the Eastern Star, an organization that essentially serves as its ladies' auxiliary (see Table 2). Freemasonry came to the colonies in the very early 1700s, and the Eastern Star was formally organized in 1876. The membership of the two groups during the twentieth century has behaved essentially the same, and the discussions of fraternal clusters begin by examining them. Unless otherwise noted, all comments refer to Freemasonry and Masonic Lodges; the Eastern Star and its chapters follow Masonry's lead closely.

The century began with 839,000 Freemasons in 12,000 lodges, each with an average of 72 members. The Craft experienced nearly continuous growth until 1928. During this period, the average annual initiation rate was 8%, with a real annual growth of 5%, and a computed annual loss of 3%. Put another way, the typical American lodge of 72 initiated about 6 members in 1900 and lost just over 2 (due to all causes). By 1930 it had 214 members with 17 initiations and 7 losses. The year 1920, just after World War I, stands out during this period with an initiation rate of 11%.

It is worth noting that several years before the Depression, Masonic membership growth was flat, and in fact peaked about two years before the stock market crash of 1929. From this peak before the Depression until 1941, the last year of membership decline, Freemasonry lost close to 25% of its membership. The number of Eastern Star chapters declined by 10%, and so it can be inferred that about 10% of Masonic Lodges also went dark during this period. The typical lodge declined from 214 to 160 members.

In 1942, after the United States was beginning to recover from the devastating effects of the Depression and as it started producing for World War II, Freemasonry began nearly two decades of continual growth. By 1959, the number of Freemasons in the United States peaked at 4,100,000, an increase of 67% from 1941, and the average lodge now had 259 members!

Table 2: Freemason Cluster

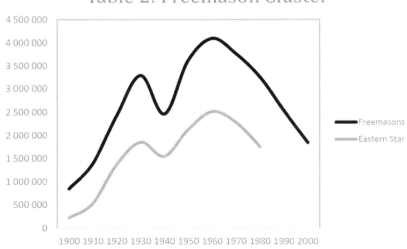

TABLE 2. Freemason Cluster, 1900–2000

Then, in 1959, Freemasonry stopped growing, and began a slow, steady decline of a little more than 1% per year to today. By 1980, the average lodge in the United States had 213 members, initiated 6 and lost 8. The computed loss during this period, interestingly enough, was about 3% per year, the same as during the first 30 years of growth in the century. Obviously the annual initiation rate is much lower, 2% now versus 8% then. In 1980, Freemasonry's membership was almost 4 times as large as in 1900, and 80% of its 1959 high.

The Eastern Star began the century with 26% of Masonry's membership, and by 1920 had grown to 59% of it. Since then, its membership has remained in about the same relationship to Masonry's. It peaked at 61% in 1970 and was about 53% in 1980.

Odd Fellows

The second fraternal cluster to be considered is led by the Independent Order of Odd Fellows, and includes the Patriarchs, the Patriarchs Militant, the Rebekah (all Odd Fellow auxiliaries), and the Knights of Pythias (see Table 3). Like Freemasonry, the Odd Fellows were a British import to America but began in Baltimore in 1819. The Rebekah degree was organized in 1851 as perhaps the first female auxiliary to an American fraternal order, and in 1885 the "higher" degrees of the Patriarchs and the Patriarchs Militant were added to the Odd Fellows' constellation. In 1864, the Knights of Pythias, an entirely native organization, was formed to help heal the wounds of the Civil War. Unless otherwise noted, all comments that follow refer to Odd Fellowship and its lodges. The other groups follow the Odd Fellows' lead closely.

Odd Fellowship started the century like nearly every other American fraternity: with strong and steady growth. In 1900, it had 870,000 members and an average lodge of 76 members that initiated 7 and lost 4 per year. Its growth stopped in 1920, a full ten years before the Depression, with 1,736,000 members and an average lodge of 112. During these two decades of increase, the average initiation rate was 9% per year, the real annual growth was 4%, and the computed annual loss was 5%. In the ten years before the Depression, the Odd Fellows lost 420,000 members, a decline of 24%. By 1940, Odd Fellowship had declined to 666,000, with an average lodge down to 70 members, a frightening 62% loss from its 1920 high. (By comparison, Freemasonry in 1940 had declined only 24% from its pre-Depression high.)

Table 3: Odd Fellows Cluster

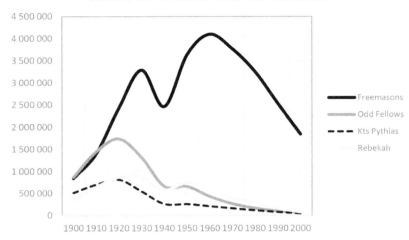

TABLE 3. Odd Fellows Cluster, 1900–2000

In 1945, an interesting event occurred: Rebekah membership rose above that of the Odd Fellows. The Rebekahs grew a total of 18% from 1940 to 1955,when numerical decline began again for them. During the same period, Odd Fellowship's decline eased momentarily (and almost imperceptibly) around 1950. Except for this brief respite, Odd Fellowship has declined about 4% per year since 1920. An average initiation rate of 4% has been maintained, but the computed loss is 8% (compared with Freemasonry's 3%). The average lodge that had 112 members in 1920 had 40 members in 1980. Odd Fellow membership in 1980 was 19% of its 1900 membership, and about 10% of its 1920 peak.

Scottish Rite

The Ancient and Accepted Scottish Rite of Freemasonry was founded in 1801, and heads the third cluster of fraternities. This group includes the Shriners (Ancient Arabic Order, Nobles of the Mystic Shrine), founded in 1872; the Knights of Columbus, founded in 1882; and the Elks (Benevolent and Protective Order of Elks), founded in 1868 (see Table 4). Shrine membership was limited until 2000 to 32° Scottish Rite Masons or Knights Templar from the Masonic York Rite (discussed in the next cluster). The Elks are included on the basis of very limited data, national totals for only the decades from 1930 to 1970. The Elks' larger lodges produce an organizational structure similar to the Scottish Rite and the Shrine, and the Elks' emphasis on social activities parallels the Shrine. The Knights of Columbus, the largest of the four organizations, should lead this cluster, but initiations are not included in the Knights' annual summaries, unlike the Scottish Rite. Thus all comments that follow are for the Scottish Rite because of the more complete data available. The Scottish Rite data refers to the most widely distributed local units, the Lodges of Perfection, which confer 4° through 14°.

The most aggressive fraternal growth seen at the beginning of the century came in this cluster. In 1900 the Scottish Rite had 40,000 members and grew continually to 590,000 by 1929. (The Shrine and the Knights of Columbus stopped growing about 1926.) The average growth of the Scottish Rite was 13% per year, the actual growth was 9%, and the computed loss was nearly 4%, about the same as the 3% for Freemasonry. In 1900, the average Lodge of Perfection had 241 members, initiated 32, and lost only 9; by 1930 that lodge had grown to 2,167. With constant, dramatic growth, that certainly must have been a heady time to have been involved with the Scottish Rite.

Renewed growth for each of these groups began about 1940. In the fifteen-year period of decline for the Shrine and the Knights, they lost about 45% of their membership. During its ten years of decline, the Scottish Rite lost 33% of its members. By 1945, five years into the recovery, the annual growth rate for its Lodges of Perfection had returned to 13.0%, or 250 new members a year for each lodge!

Table 4: Scottish Rite Cluster

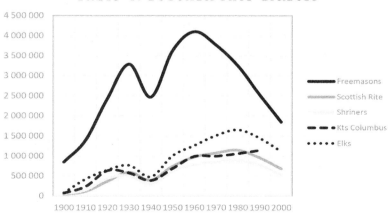

TABLE 4: Scottish Rite Cluster, 1900–2000

From 1940 to 1980, the Scottish Rite had uninterrupted growth, from 396,000 to 1,150,000, a total increase of 190%. Although, from 1960, the date of Masonic membership decline, to 1980, the annual growth rate was 1%, the average growth rate was 4% and the computed loss was 3%, about the same loss as in the beginning of the twentieth century. Membership in the Scottish Rite peaked about 1980 at 29 times its 1900 level, and has been declining slowly since. Shrine membership reached its high point a little before 1980, with 16 times its 1900 level. The Knights of Columbus, in contrast, suffered a 2% loss from 1965 to 1975, but had a remarkable 7% total growth from 1975 to 1980.

York Rite

The fourth cluster is composed of Royal Arch Masons, Royal and Select Masters, and the Knights Templar (see Table 5). These three loosely cooperating organizations are known as the York Rite of Freemasonry, though the title American Rite is perhaps more accurate. Royal Arch Masonry came to America with Freemasonry during the colonial period, and was worked by at least 1753. Masonic Templary seems to have come later, about 1770, and Councils of Royal and Select Masters came later still, about 1800. A Christian Royal Arch Mason may become a Knight Templar, and the Royal and Select Master degrees are encouraged options for Royal Arch Masons. A Knight Templar may join the Shrine, as may a 32° Scottish Rite Mason. Unless noted, all figures refer to Chapters of Royal Arch Masons.

Membership growth for Royal Arch Masonry at the beginning of the century was much the same as that for Freemasonry and Odd Fellowship, though quite a bit less than that for the Scottish Rite. From 1900 to 1926, Royal Arch membership grew from 223,000 to 908,000. The average initiation rate was 8% per year, the growth rate was 6%, and the computed loss was an almost negligible 2%. The average Royal Arch Chapter in 1900 had 86 members, initiated 7, and lost only 2; and by 1925 it had grown to 233, with 18 initiations, and 4 losses. Commanderies of Knights Templar had about 30 more members than Royal Arch Chapters during this period. Then followed a fifteen-year period of decline, though the loss from 1925 to 1930 was only slight.

By 1940, Royal Arch membership had dropped by 47%, and an average chapter had only 148. From 1942 to 1957, Royal Arch Masonry grew from 477,000 to 705,000, with an average initiation rate of 5%, a growth rate of 3%, and still a small computed loss of 2%. However, from 1957 to the present, the Royal Arch has been declining at a rate of 1% per year, with an average initiation rate of 3%, and a computed loss of 4%. In 1980 the Royal Arch was twice its 1900 level, and 55% of its 1957 peak. In 1960, an average commandery had 43 more members than an average chapter, but by 1980 there were only 15 more members.

Table 5: York Rite Cluster

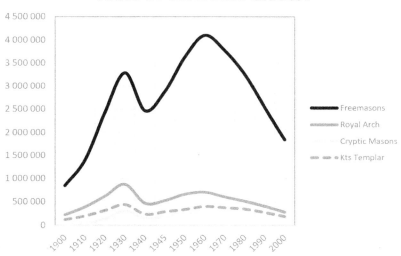

TABLE 5: York Rite Cluster, 1900–2000

It is worth noting a subtle change affecting the relationship of Knights Templar and Royal Arch Masons. Knights Templar draw their initiates from Master Masons who have become Royal Arch Masons. In 1900, 54% of Royal Arch Masons were Knights Templar, and this percentage remained fairly constant until 1955. From 1955 to 1980 the number of Royal Arch Masons who went on to become Knights steadily climbed from 54% to 68%. Thus "York Rite Unity," which has proved so impossible to achieve through de jure methods, may become a de facto reality.

Why It Happened

A fraternity will often delude itself into believing that initiates seek membership because of a desire to attain the knowledge contained within the inner sanctum of its temple. To use the time honored language of most

Masonic membership petitions, a candidate "seriously declares, upon his honour, that, unbiased by friends, and uninfluenced by mercenary motives, [he] freely and voluntarily offers [himself] a candidate for the mysteries of Masonry."[5] Only during serious soul searching will Masons (and others) admit that a very few men join for "unworthy motives" (such as business contacts, Shrine membership, political benefits, and so on).

In fact, a majority of applicants probably seek Masonic and other fraternal memberships for reasons little related to the organizations' noble purposes. While the desire for a satisfying philosophy of life certainly attracted and continues to attract new members to fraternities, other perhaps "baser" motives cannot be dismissed. Alvin Schmidt in his encyclopedic work, *Fraternal Organizations,* gives four basic reasons that he believes influence people to join a fraternity: social integration, religion and morality, economic security, and social prestige.[6] To this list must be added community involvement.

The organizations considered in this study effectively drew their memberships in the twentieth century from native-born Americans. The Knights of Columbus were a likely exception, however, probably drawing some of their membership from the large Catholic immigrant population. Thus there was little impact from the social integration factor on these groups, which was so important in ethnic organizations such as the Order of Sons of Italy or the Ancient Order of Hibernians. However, other factors surely were of critical importance.

The matter of economic security must rank as one of the great reasons to join a fraternal order near the turn of the century. It is not by mere chance or pure altruism that so many orphanages and old-age homes were built by Masons, Odd Fellows, Pythians, and others. There was a period, not so long ago, when limited healthcare, inadequate or nonexistent insurance, and an almost total lack of industrial safety made orphanages a desirable benefit of fraternal membership. Further, the absence of Social Security and pensions made the availability of retirement homes a critical safety net.

As increased job benefits, improved medical care, and expanded government assistance have removed citizens' worries, so these changes have di-

---

5 Thomas Smith Webb, *Illustrations of Masonry* (Salem, MA: Cushing and Appleton, 1816), 29.

6 Schmidt, *Fraternal Organizations,* 16–19.

minished many of the tangible benefits of fraternal membership. Charles W. Ferguson neatly summed up this direct appeal of fraternal membership:

> There can be no doubt, however, that the emphasis on the cash-and-carry benefits of brotherhood attracted swarms of members—good as well as bad. The lodge was a sanctuary which would protect them from the preying beasts of insecurity and want. The [economic] appeals of the lodge may seem to us quaint and over-drawn today, but they were addressed to realities on a plane on which men lived.[7]

An ironic example of the problems associated with luring members with the promise of economic security is given by the Odd Fellows. In 1888, their *Manual of the Work and Usages of the Order* stated "All [Subordinate Lodges] must pay some stipulated weekly [sick] benefits. Benefits are a right and not a charity."[8] Eventually, Odd Fellowship realized that emphasizing benefits was attracting members who had no more than a passing interest in the Order itself.

"In 1926 the Grand Sire of the [Independent Order of Odd Fellows] pronounced against all benefits and deplored the type of person who had been roped in by promise of pecuniary reward, but by then the damage seems to have been done."[9] The increased availability of these social services from the 1920s more than coincidentally matched the decline of American fraternalism.

The issues of religion and morality have been central to fraternities in general and Freemasonry in particular. For example, in describing the settlement of the Louisiana Purchase in the beginning of the nineteenth century, Ray Vaughn Denslow pointed out that "Masonry had preceded the Church ... the result was that many [of the new settlers] were compelled to secure most of their religious solace from reading the family Bible and in attendance at the local lodge, causing many to regard the Masonic Fraternity as a religion rather than a guide post to religion."[10] With the declining influence

---

7   Charles W. Ferguson, *Fifty Million Brothers* (New York: Farrar & Rinehart, Inc., 1937), 229.

8   Theo. A. Ross, *Odd Fellowship: Its History and Manual* (New York: M. W. Hazen Co., 1888), 510.

9   Ferguson, *Fifty Million Brothers*, 228.

10 Ray Vaughn Denslow, *Territorial Masonry* (Washington: Masonic Service Association

and importance of religion in American life, and the increasing secularization of society, it is not surprising that organizations perceived by the public as being quasi-religious in nature have less and less appeal.

The matter of social prestige is difficult to measure, but it was certainly at least as important as economic security. Alvin Schmidt precisely captures the notion:

> A couple of decades before and after 1900, when there were no automobiles, radios, television sets, or movie theaters, the fraternal organization often was the only place in which individuals could experience social prestige or feel important. Numerous lodge groups enabled their members to adorn themselves in colorful regalia and then participate in public events. Such participation was especially important in small, rural towns. Fraternal members could impress their fellow townsmen, particularly nonmembers, in that by belonging to certain fraternal orders they were different and distinctive. ...
>
> But as American society increasingly became urbanized, the social advantage of belonging to a fraternal order lost much of its appeal in the context of anonymity. When someone is unknown among large numbers of people, who is there to impress? Thus, the present decline in membership of most fraternal societies is caused not only by the lack of organizational change ... but also by the inability of fraternal orders to provide social prestige for their members as they once did.[11]

Paradoxically, Freemasonry and the other fraternities seem to have been hurt by their very popularity and success. As more people joined, it was more difficult to maintain the image of an exclusive group with limited membership.

"In contrast to the civic clubs, for example, Masonry was clearly less selective. Similarly, the large size of urban lodges precluded the sense of fraternity that earlier lodge life may have been able to establish."[12]

---

of the US, 1925), 5.

11 Schmidt, 17, 18.

12 Lynn Dumenil, *Freemasonry and American Culture, 1890–1920* (Princeton: Princeton University Press, 1984), 218–19.

Another important and overlooked factor on declining prestige, particularly with Freemasonry, is a static dues structure coupled with rampant inflation. There was a period when becoming a Freemason involved a considerable financial commitment. In Missouri around 1929, the cost of becoming just a Knight Templar (including a uniform) was $125![13] Freemasonry appears to have built its financial house upon the sandy notion that continuous, strong growth (seen in five of the six decades from 1900 to 1960) would keep a steady stream of initiation fees flowing into the treasury. Thus, rather than tax themselves by raising dues to keep pace with inflation, the Craft myopically relied on initiation fees and its burgeoning membership's dues to meet expenses.

This worked quite well, as long as growth continued. However, as initiation rates declined, Grand Lodges refused to raise initiation fees for fear of discouraging applicants. Further, annual dues have not risen because of the burden they may put upon superannuated members (who may also belong to the Shrine and York or Scottish Rites). The unintended result of this cowardice is that becoming a Freemason is now within the financial grasp of any working-class citizen, and thus lacking the prestige associated (perhaps wrongly) with an expensive purchase. An initiation fee that may have equaled a week's wages at the beginning of the century now equals a family dinner at a very nice restaurant.

Finally, community involvement must be considered a significant attraction of fraternities. In an earlier, simpler time when many Americans lived, were educated, and worked within a few miles of their birthplaces, these groups played a vital part in community activities. Members of fraternal organizations were the quintessence of civic responsibility. Their direct charitable support—perhaps a cord of firewood or financial support during hard times or funeral arrangements—provided essential services. For people without telephones or cars, the lodge meeting was an important opportunity to keep track of friends and news. When there were few radios or televisions or theaters, the simple pleasure of talking with lodge brothers on meeting night provided unparalleled entertainment. If fine restaurants and comfortable clubs were dimly distant delights, then the simple furnishings and modest fare of the lodge provided accessible gratification.

---

13 Ray Vaughn Denslow, *Is Anything Wrong with Templarism?* (N.p. [Missouri?]: N.d. [1929?]), 9.

Lodges today are prepared to meet the needs they always have, with the methods that have always worked for them. However, the needs of society, that they hope so desperately to serve, have changed. The tightly knit local community that once was so ably assisted by its fraternal organizations has dispersed and disintegrated almost beyond recognition. Where once it was easy for lodges to know the needs of their members' families, it is now hard for lodges to even know their members. This then is what has happened to the community involvement of American fraternalism: a gradual diminishing of the need for fraternal services, to the point that fewer and fewer are attracted to these increasingly quaint organizations.

Summary

Freemasonry, the oldest and most prestigious of American fraternities, enjoyed steady growth until shortly before 1930. Its Depression decline of 25% was the smallest of any other fraternity, and is probably explained by the fact that it drew its membership from the professional and business classes more than other organizations. In 1940, with a sudden return to exuberant health, certain fundamental changes seem to have occurred in the membership of the Craft. At that time, status seekers had abandoned lodges for ever more exclusive domains, such as country clubs.[14]

Into this vacuum moved a new class of initiate, no less sincere or principled than his earlier brothers, but slightly lower on the socioeconomic status ladder; the working classes replaced the professional and business classes. A 1976 survey of Kansas Masons discovered that "Masons who joined prior to 1955 were 33% more likely to have managerial or professional jobs and 19% more likely to have obtained a college degree."[15] In 1960, Freemasonry reached its peak membership, and since then it has been steadily, slowly, and inexorably declining. It is probable that men who at the beginning of the century would have been Odd Fellows today become Masons, while yesterday's Masons are now in a country club.

The Independent Order of Odd Fellows and the Knights of Pythias have suffered the worst of any fraternal organization during the last eighty years. If nobility of purpose or height of ideals or extent of charity were the basis

---

14 Noel Gist, "Secret Societies: A Cultural Study of Fraternalism in the United States," *University of Missouri Studies* 15, no. 1 (Oct. 1940): 44.

15 John Wilson, "Voluntary Associations and Civil Religion: The Case of Freemasonry," *Review of Religious Research* 22, no 2. (1980): 127–28.

of success, then each order would today be models of health. Looking at the start of the twentieth century, no one could have guessed the calamity of the present. The Odd Fellows grew steadily until 1920, and then began a nearly fatal decline; the decline from 1920 to 1935 alone exceeded all the growth from 1900 to 1920.

Odd Fellows were more likely to be drawn from the working class than Freemasons. John H. White, Grand Sire of the Odd Fellows in 1888, said that "American Odd Fellowship is composed of the great middle, industrial classes almost exclusively; Masonry [is composed] of all grades of society, from the titled and wealthy of this and foreign lands, to the humblest laborer. ..."[16] The heavily emphasized economic benefits of membership obviously appealed to the working class, though this appeal ultimately may have backfired. Members began drifting away in the early 1920s, coincidentally as health and life insurance became more widely available. Then the Depression, with particularly crushing effects on the working class, seems to have delivered the knockout punch. It is very likely that the much touted benefits could not be delivered (for reasons completely beyond the Odd Fellows' control), and that may have left bitter residual feelings towards the Order.

By 1940, when Freemasonry rebounded with vigor, Odd Fellowship, which had lost 62% of its membership and 38% of its lodges, continued to decline. The average Odd Fellow Lodge now had only 70 members, a size probably too small to support the activities required to sustain a modern fraternity. Finally, working-class men, the Odd Fellows' traditional membership base, began to join the more prestigious Freemasonry in greater numbers. There was a brief pause in decline around 1950, and since then a steady, discouraging loss of 4% per year.

The Scottish Rite cluster has fared the best of all fraternities this century. Absolutely stunning real growth of 9% marked the first three decades. Then the Depression caused a 33% drop for the Scottish Rite, and 45% for the Shrine and the Knights of Columbus. The Shrine probably lost more because its activities were almost purely social and because its dues would be in addition to Masonic plus York or Scottish Rite dues. The Knights' loss may be due to the fact that many Catholics at that time were less wealthy and recent immigrants. Further, the Knights' greatest decline came from their "Associate Members" who enjoyed only social benefits. Knights with

---

16 Ross, *Odd Fellowship*, 2.

life insurance increased from 28% to 53% of the membership from 1920 to 1940, showing that economic necessity won over social activity.

In 1940, the renewed growth of the Scottish Rite was again greater than that of any other fraternity, though its growth gradually slowed until 1980, when it too began a gradual decline. It is rather remarkable that the Scottish Rite and the Shrine, both drawing their membership from Masons, were able to continue growth for nearly twenty years after Freemasonry stopped growing. This probably indicates that an ever-larger number of Masons are joining for Shrine membership. The Shrine is acutely aware of its diminishing pool of possible members, and has tried recently to drop Masonic membership as a requirement to allow aggressive recruitment of new Shriners.

Royal Arch Masonry began the century with the same real growth as Freemasonry, about 5%. However the Depression caused a 51% Royal Arch decline, versus 33% for the Scottish Rite and 25% for Freemasonry. After 1940, the York Rite has done consistently worse than Freemasonry: its recovery was less dramatic, its membership peaked five years earlier in 1955, and its annual loss has been greater.

Some of the problems of Royal Arch Masonry and the York Rite may be traced to their organizational structure. Their local bodies are smaller and more widely dispersed than the large, urban Valleys of the Scottish Rite. As the United States has shifted from a rural to an urban population, the Scottish Rite has benefited. York Rite membership, requiring two or three entirely separate dues payments, can be more expensive than Scottish Rite membership. The Scottish Rite has almost infinite flexibility in conferring its degrees, while the York Rite can only do it one way, and rather slowly at that. Finally, the Knights Templar are stuck with a Victorian uniform that does little to draw new members to its ranks, and may in fact actively repel them.

Not only has the uniform hurt Knights Templar, but it has also been a burden to the uniformed ranks of other fraternities: the Patriarchs Militant, the Knights of Pythias, and the fourth degree Knights of Columbus. At one time, these military organizations captured the fancy of the public, and provided an alluring appeal to fraternal membership.

> Caparisoned in accordance with the demands of Victorian taste, for years [they] served their gilded purpose [of drumming up a crowd, passing out sample impressions, and presenting their Orders often and favorably to the public mind]. In time their appeal

dimmed, for the simple reason that styles changed. At first they changed imperceptibly and then shockingly, so that the gorgeous apparel which had dazzled a generation accustomed to horsehair sofas, rococo architecture, high bicycles, front doors with colored glass around the edges, antimacassars, and elaborate cruets, grew less and less dumfounding and [organizations] once bathed in splendor became dated.[17]

In short, the twentieth century has not been kind to Freemasonry and American fraternities. They have bravely maintained their ideals and have blindly continued their procedures, unable to distinguish the essential from the ephemeral. Their operations are virtually the same as a century ago, but they do not want to admit that American society has changed. "[They] are like small children whimpering during a thunderstorm: unaware of what is really happening, unsure of what to do, and frightened by the apparent chaos of nature."[18] It is evident that changes are necessary, but no one knows what they should be, because it is so difficult and painful for fraternities to separate form from substance.

A Church with a failing membership will consider any explanation for its decline, except that its tenets are false or that its dogma is wrong. Similarly, fraternities equate suggestions of change with doubts of their fundamental, fraternal principles and mount a tenacious defense against all perceived attacks. Thus, in the context of this fierce protection of organizational *raison d'être*, to intimate that procedural changes may be appropriate is to advocate the abandonment of the ritual or to deny the principles of the order, to even hint that the Emperor has no clothes is to conspire against the state.

Fraternal change is inevitable; the only question is whether it will be planned or accidental. Time alone will provide the answer.

REFERENCES

Anderson, Albin C. "Summary of Candidates and Membership—1924 to 1951 Inclusive." Manuscript, New York, 1952.

---

17 Ferguson, 230–31.

18 S. Brent Morris, "The Siren Song of Solicitation," *The Royal Arch Mason Magazine* 14, no. 6 (Summer 1983): 167.

————. "Statistical Summary—Fiscal Year 1960." Manuscript, New York, 1961.

————. "Statistical Summary—Fiscal Year 1964." Manuscript, New York, 1965.

Carnahan, James R. *Pythian Knighthood: Its History and Literature.* Cincinnati: Pettibone Mfg. Co., 1888.

Denslow, Ray Vaughn. *Territorial Masonry.* Washington: Masonic Service Association of the US, 1925.

————. *Is Anything Wrong with Templarism?* N.p. (Missouri?): N.d. (1929?).

Dumenil, Lynn. *Freemasonry and American Culture, 1890–1920.* Princeton: Princeton University Press, 1984.

Ferguson, Charles W. *Fifty Million Brothers.* New York: Farrar & Rinehart, 1937.

Gist, Noel. *Secret Societies: A Cultural Study of Fraternalism in the United States.* University of Missouri Studies, 1940, 9–176.

Jones, Preston. *A Texas Trilogy.* New York: Hill and Ward, 1976.

Merz, Charles. "Sweet Land of Secrecy." *Harper's Monthly Magazine* 154 (1927): 329–34.

Morris, S. Brent. "A Fraternal Abstract of the United States: 1900–1980." Manuscript, Columbia, MD, 1981.

————. "Trends Affecting American Freemasonry." *The Philalethes* 35, no. 2 (Apr. 1982): 16–17.

————. "The Public Image of Freemasonry." *The Royal Arch Mason Magazine* 14, no. 4 (Winter 1982): 105–11.

————. "The Siren Song of Solicitation." *The Royal Arch Mason Magazine* 14, no. 6 (Summer 1983): 163–68.

Ross, Theo. A. *Odd Fellowship: Its History and Manual.* New York: M. W. Hazen Co., 1888.

Schmidt, Alvin J. *Fraternal Organizations.* Westport, CT: Greenwood Press, 1980.

———. *Oligarchy in Fraternal Organizations.* Detroit: Gale Research Co., 1973.

——— and Nicholas Babchuk. "Trends in U.S. Fraternal Associations in the Twentieth Century." *Voluntary Action Research*: 1973. Edited by David Horton. Lexington Books, 1973.

Voorhis, Harold van Buren. *Masonic Organizations and Allied Orders and Degrees.* New York: Press of Henry Emmerson, 1952.

Webb, Thomas Smith. *Illustrations of Masonry.* Salem, MA: Cushing and Appleton, 1816.

Wilson, John. "Voluntary Association and Civil Religion: The Case of Masonry." *Review of Religious Research* 22, no. 2 (1980): 125–36.

APPENDIX

US Fraternal Memberships, 1900–2000

The data that follows represents figures from the forty-eight continental states and the District of Columbia. For each year are listed local units ("Lodges" or "Chapters," etc.), initiates, and total membership, including the initiates and less all losses. For the Knights of Columbus, there are no figures for initiations, but the membership is divided between "Insurance" and "Associate" members. The Rebekah gives initiates and members by men and women. In some cases, estimations been made, and are indicated by italics (for example, many state Grand Councils of Royal and Select Masters do not belong to the General Grand Council, and so do not report their membership figures in the national body's annual transactions).

1	FREEMASONS			EASTERN STAR		
Year	Lodges	Initiates	Members	Chapters	Initiates	Members
1900	11,655	51,346	843,380	3,439	24,923	219,580
1905		55,826	1,091,782			
1910	13,617	84,308	1,393,450	6,607	53,513	531,134
1915		105,814	1,739,179			
1920	15,266	279,267	2,427,713	9,746	171,701	1,375,203
1925		149,266	3,147,261			
1930		90,763	3,286,290	11,557	84,640	1,851,044
1935		42,831	2,676,730			
1940		56,786	2,462,968	10,358	52,442	1,552,239
1945		175,165	2,876,481			
1950	15,361	163,908	3,629,700	11,799	123,127	2,133,029
1955	15,662	135,021	4,003,435			
1960	15,811	104,573	4,097,603	12,410	68,504	2,516,456
1965		83,714	3,978,821			
1970		69,223	3,767,257	12,230	46,528	2,283,783
1975		68,989	3,515,614			
1980		59,011	3,249,603	8,363	38,227	1,753,020
1985		42,250	2,916,270			
1990		32,110	2,531,433			
1995		30,119	2,152,601			
2000			1,841,169			

2	ODD FELLOWS			KNIGHTS OF PYTHIAS		
Year	Lodges	Initiates	Members	Lodges	Initiates	Members
1900	11,426	87,918	870,300	6,765	52,820	511,157
1905	13,938	115,334	1,181,246	7,381	63,132	641,717
1910	16,245	115,226	1,443,897	7,728	46,328	698,203
1915	16,305	84,250	1,503,256	7,283	43,351	705,338
1920	15,485	186,360	1,736,100	6,546	85,196	811,836
1925	14,327	90,069	1,668,768	6,211	36,691	770,220
1930	12,700	33,734	1,316,032	5,254	12,116	543,305
1935	10,930	30,247	831,407	4,216	22,456	319,055
1940	9,559	31,176	665,826	3,618	18,236	260,500
1945	8,639	40,062	653,786	2,955	19,035	250,119
1950	8,072	32,923	660,161	2,656	14,547	257,327
1955	7,570	18,145	543,059	2,383	12,327	231,441
1960	6,888	10,708	431,461	2,118	8,250	208,429
1965	6,193	8,166	335,615	1,816	6,858	190,152
1970	5,475	6,833	267,012	1,498	4,097	159,631
1975	4,775	5,289	212,336	1,272	3,931	135,854
1980	4,287	3,573	164,639	1,081	2,453	113,442
1985	3,518	3,492	129,335		2,218	89,396
1990	2,948	2,758	98,512		1,361	76,023
1995	2,450	2,532	74,989		979	56,277
2000	2,026	1,785	59,892		688	42,767

2	PATRIARCHS			PATRIARCHS MILITANT		
Year	Encamps.	Initiates	Members	Cantons	Initiates	Members
1900:	2,575	14,057	129,087	502	2,038	14,326
1905:	3,142	20,030	175,843	573	2,452	18,218
1910:	3,485	19,662	207,670	802	4,096	24,344
1915:	3,313	16,357	213,131	714	2,377	27,143
1920:	3,263	61,030	292,995	692	8,083	34,180
1925:	3,385	20,339	315,716	754	2,393	36,421
1930:	3,028	7,223	230,066	718	1,234	25,375
1935:	2,650	4,263	128,350	655	1,099	16,668
1940:	2,284	4,462	92,269	592	1,219	12,980
1945:	2,041	9,683	90,674	586	3,676	16,877
1950:	2,035	6,220	102,852	682	2,194	23,371
1955:	1,957	3,382	83,904	667	937	29,795
1960:	1,805	1,956	64,244	646	762	16,643
1965:	1,588	1,311	48,325	586	510	13,603
1970:	1,409	1,050	36,517	533	409	11,084
1975:	1,220	994	28,849	504	492	9,323
1980:	1,008	590	22,046	474	232	7,466
1985	866	472	16,402	407	181	5,742
1990	728	358	12,169	348	163	4,541
1995	606	314	9,459	288	81	3,498
2000						

2	REBEKAH					
Year	Lodges	New M	New W	Total M	Total W	Members
1900:	5,458	23,186	39,188	129,387	213,563	342,950
1905:	7,136	29,128	49,822	174,740	314,177	488,917
1910:	9,085	35,261	61,263	216,937	422,269	639,206
1915:	9,132	25,946	54,599	221,101	489,490	710,591
1920:	9,002	56,524	100,521	271,504	599,820	871,324
1925:	9,579	20,941	49,863	293,089	712,242	1,005,331
1930:	9,142	8,291	26,645	221,301	653,360	874,661
1935:	8,266	3,730	18,198	124,448	493,460	617,908
1940:	7,699	3,538	32,246	89,991	488,861	578,852
1945:	7,490	6,375	43,611	108,640	557,678	666,318
1950:	7,161	6,573	40,345	102,153	646,027	748,180
1955:	7,559	2,918	20,846	83,669	598,131	681,800
1960:	7,255	2,115	5,411	66,102	526,931	593,033
1965:	6,755	1,595	11,286	51,526	443,188	494,714
1970:	6,168	1,347	9,257	39,077	354,759	393,836
1975:	5,630	1,282	9,078	32,779	309,217	341,996
1980:	5,006	849	6,107	26,391	265,441	291,832
1985	4,351	670	4,800	20,184	197,465	217,649
1990	3,612	451	2,934	14,455	146,071	160,526
1995	2,850	375	2,095	10,512	102,195	112,707
2000	2,238	219	1,374	7,617	67,814	75,431

3	SCOTTISH RITE MASONS			SHRINERS		
Year	Valleys	Initiates	Members	Temples	Initiates	Members
1900:	166	4,615	39,928	80	6,646	55,915
1905:	193	8,065	69,066	92	7,359	96,526
1910:	209	13,274	114,863	114	13,543	155,278
1915:	218	16,176	175,234	128	17,112	217,139
1920:	239	78,692	367,151	137	85,723	445,279
1925:	270	33,535	548,698	144	28,157	562,891
1930:	272	19,103	589,474	144	13,913	507,123
1935:	273	6,451	450,086	147	5,250	356,929
1940:	277	10,107	395,582	147	7,063	299,404
1945:	273	68,109	522,970	147	52,176	425,984
1950:	278	44,379	744,108	150	41,796	619,831
1955:	287	45,629	890,100	154	40,471	738,972
1960:	293	40,531	973,739	154	31,651	786,266
1965:	296	41,876	1,029,757	156	34,737	808,164
1970:	300	45,117	1,078,251	158	37,843	849,228
1975:	297	48,468	1,128,561	164	41,061	896,888
1980:	305	37,750	1,147,584	165	29,075	889,825
1985	306	28.356	1,125,884			884,441
1990	304	19.408	957,382			774,184
1995	302	15.508	799,418			633,762
2000			679,163			528,978

3	KNIGHTS OF COLUMBUS				ELKS
Year	Councils	Insurance	Associate	Members	Members
1900:	534	30,436	38,265	68,701	77,351
1905:		43,315	82,569	125,884	
1910:	1,386	76,366	158,999	235,365	419,319
1915:	1,635	108,266	218,526	326,792	442,658
1920:	1,880	184,302	445,241	629,543	645,678
1925:	2,202	229,254	470,231	699,495	832,083
1930:	2,297	242,489	328,998	571,487	761,461
1935:	2,256	220,612	196,868	417,480	468,043
1940:	2,253	207,352	175,869	383,221	475,599
1945:	2,281	203,994	264,331	468,325	705,570
1950:	2,549	263,468	421,218	684,686	1,004,985
1955:	2,985	295,245	505,241	800,486	1,149,613
1960:	3,745	379,851	605,644	985,495	1,260,007
1965:	4,237	400,665	612,163	1,012,828	1,361,455
1970:	4,432	387,614	607,596	995,210	1,508,050
1975:	4,587	376,365	615,904	992,269	1,582,735
1980:	5,121	393,276	665,730	1,059,006	1,649,267
1985:	5,846	447,263	696,046	1,143,309	1,594,954
1990:	6,561	431,724	709,305	1,141,029	1,448,043
1995:	7,255	446,487	710,089	1,156,576	1,282,017
2000:					1,113,713

4	ROYAL ARCH MASONS			ROYAL & SELECT		
Year	Chapters	Initiates	Members	Councils	Initiates	Members
1900	2,879	15.268	223,391	392	2,273	32,548
1905	3,217	25,503	296,290			
1910	3,636	32,568	385,936	578	5,577	55,277
1915	3,539	27,683	465,894			
1920	3,656	71,176	615,948	799	25,416	136,765
1925	3,996	44,097	918,925		17,745	329,993
1930	3,962	19,772	873,302		7,680	311,351
1935	3,750	6,502	600,348		2,483	203,797
1940	3,427	10,836	465,705		4,099	153,818
1945	3.333	47,433	521,016		20,984	180,261
1950	3,391	37,095	658,956	1,296	17,545	250,396
1955	3,406	29,699	707,877	378	15,221	285,301
1960	3,401	23,683	700,596	1,445	15,042	302,114
1965	3,352	16,914	649,743	1,489	72,854	305,356
1970	2,777	12,514	598,464			
1975			557,230		10,177	211,028
1980			507,724			
1985						
1990						
1995						
2000						

4	KNIGHTS TEMPLAR		
Year	Commds.	Initiates	Members
1900	1,036	7,008	120,710
1905	1,139	12,372	155,474
1910	1,291	13,023	198,964
1915	1,386	13,929	236,726
1920	1,496	43,206	313,667
1925	1,676	22,686	446,601
1930	1,693	10,657	434,444
1935	1,653	2,768	311,469
1940	1,587	12,701	237,250
1945	1,577	26,247	286,526
1950	1,597	20,433	334,647
1955	1,606	18,628	378,106
1960	1,609	17,300	395,427
1965	1,599	14,239	384,857
1970	1,576	11,924	369,890
1975	1,549	13,797	357,038
1980	1,514	11,710	343,610
1985	1,481	9,492	315,760
1990	1,440	6,443	272,575
1995	1,381	5,284	226,075
2000	1,340	4,792	189,146

Masonic Membership Myths

Myths are comforting stories told by primitive societies to provide order for the world—to explain the unexplainable. Even if nature is frightening, myths establish a framework in which she is understandable. Today, myths provide assurance to children that many of life's mysteries have benign explanations: thunder is caused by celestial bowling; the Sandman puts "sand" in our eyes when we sleep; and Masonic membership is momentarily declining for simple, well understood reasons.

Just as we abandon childhood's monsters when we mature, so should we replace Masonic membership myths when we analyze the data. However, the same simple satisfactions that draw children to fairy tales continue to draw Masonic leaders to painless theories—theories that are dangerously wrong. The facts are available for study, the explanations are complex, and the solutions are only dimly perceived, but that is no excuse for turning aside from truth.

Masonic Membership from 1870

The chart shows 3° and 14° membership in the United States from 1870 to 1987 (Lodge of Perfection data is used as these bodies have the widest distribution in the Scottish Rite). From 1870 to 1928, the Blue Lodges had strong, continuous growth. Up to 1905, the growth was about 2.3% per year, and from 1905 to 1928 the annual increase was 5%. In 1928, a year before the stock market crash, 3° membership peaked at 3.3 million and began to fall. The Depression accelerated this decline, and we lost 26% of our brothers before bottoming out in 1941 at 2.5 million and then rebounding with vigor. The boom lasted seventeen years to 1959; Blue Lodge membership has since steadily declined to 33% of its peak. Scottish Rite membership grew faster than Craft Masonry in the beginning, declined 36% in the 1930s, rebounded faster, peaked in 1978, and has suffered total losses of about 5% since then.

Myth 1: Our current losses are part of the cyclic nature of Masonry.

There is no cyclical pattern to Masonic membership! Except for the losses around the 1930s, Freemasonry enjoyed constant growth to 1958, with no significant fluctuations. Our rules, customs, and expectations have been

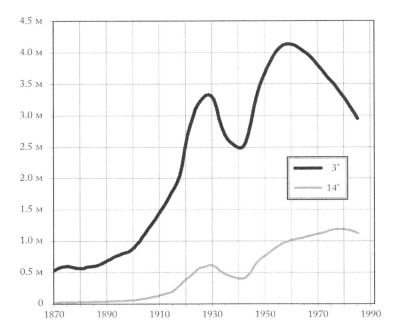

United States 3° and 14° Membership, 1870–2010

based on exceptional growth for 74 out of the last 117 years. Prior to 1959, Masonic leaders did not have to manage shrinking budgets, failing lodges, or decreasing petitions—health, growth, and prosperity seemed to be our birthright. Lodges were exhorted to do what they had always done, and then all would be right in the world.

Since then the game has changed, the ball is different, and the home court advantage has gone, but we still try to play by the same rules. If we assume that it takes Masonic leaders twenty-five to thirty years to progress to the Grand East, then we are just now seeing leaders who served during a period when fraternal membership was not a societal norm. These are men who should understand that the methods that served the Craft a century ago miss the mark today. Perhaps they will have the courage to look to innovative solutions.

Myth 2. Masonry flourishes during times of war and crisis.

Like the best of myths, this one has a grain of truth in it, but not much more. Just following World War I (1914–1918), the initiation rate was over 10% per year, twice the average for a typical four-year period. Looking at the chart, however, there is no noticeable change in membership totals around 1920, and in fact the growth began slowing in 1925. The tremendous growth associated with World War II (1941–1945) can be explained as easily by the general economic recovery after the Depression as by anything else. Membership growth began slowing during and after the Korean Conflict (1950–1953), we were well into our current period of decline during the Vietnam Conflict (1965–1974), and there was no change in membership growth during the Spanish-American War (1898–1899). The only non-wartime crisis that affected Masonic membership was the Depression, and then our membership dropped.

Myth 3. The Depression was the only thing that stopped our growth before 1959.

Here is another myth with a grain of truth. Certainly the Depression stopped Masonic growth, just as it stopped everything else in its path. However, Masonic membership had peaked in 1928 and was already declining before the Depression. In fact, some states had started experiencing decline before 1925. The Odd Fellows, the Knights of Pythias, and other fraternities started losing members in 1920, a full ten years before the economic ravages of the 1930s. Fraternal membership was declining because it had stopped being the social norm, but this decline was hidden by losses caused by the Depression. Through the rose-tinted glasses of hindsight, it's easy to overlook the problems that started before 1929.

Myth 4: If we just keep doing business as usual, everything will get better.

This is about as effective as holding your breath when walking past a cemetery. During the last thirty years we have valiantly maintained the status quo while we have lost one-third of our members. Many American cities have dying department stores that desperately cling to their formerly prestigious locations and to their time-honored methods. These bastions of antiquated commerce did not see their customers moving to the suburbs, they could not imagine that "downtown" would ever cease to be a social and fashion center, and they insisted on doing business as usual. The results are sad, abandoned businesses—faded reminders of an earlier, elegant way of life. At times it seems that Freemasonry shares the management philosophy of these dinosaurs of marketing.

We cannot continue to believe that rules, language, and procedures that were adapted for 1850–1900 are necessarily appropriate for 2000. The time has come for careful self-examination to separate form from function and to distinguish between the essential from the ephemeral. The Masonic Renewal Task Force, sponsored by the Scottish and York Rites, the Shrine, and the Masonic Service Association, has found that among men under 40 substantial interest in groups like Freemasonry exists. However, these men are partners with their wives in two-worker families, more than half claim to have at most five spare hours a month, and they seek family-oriented activities. We can take advantage of this opportunity, but only if we are willing to adapt to our times, just as our earlier brethren did.

Change is coming to American Freemasonry; the only question is whether it will be planned or accidental. Time alone will provide the answer.

References

1. Masonic Renewal Task Force. *American Male Attitudes and Behavior Towards Joining Freemasonry.* Silver Spring, MD: Masonic Service Association, 1989.

2. Masonic Service Association. "Masonic Membership Totals Since 1924." Silver Spring, MD: Masonic Service Association, 1989.

3. ———. *Comparison Statistics.* Washington: Masonic Service Association, 1948.

4. Morris, S. Brent. "Boom to Bust in the Twentieth Century." The 1988 Anson Jones Lecture. Texas Lodge of Research, March 19, 1988.

5. Voorhis, Harold V. B. *Masonic Organizations and Allied Orders and Degrees.* New York: Press of Henry Emmerson, 1952.

First published: *The Scottish Rite Journal* 97, no. 11 (November 1990)

Voting With Their Feet

I love humanity. It's people I can't stand.
—Linus van Pelt, *Peanuts, Charles Schulz*

A low rumble of thunder is an early warning sign of a rainstorm. Anyone working in a well-run building should be familiar with the clanging of the fire alarms. Few have heard, but nearly everyone knows about, the distinctive warning sound of a rattlesnake. These are all obvious warnings of impending danger, warnings that we have been trained to heed or face grave consequences. Other warning signs are subtler. Carbon monoxide and radon are colorless, odorless, fatal gasses that endanger—one killing quickly and the other over decades. And thousands of deformed frogs have been found in Minnesota and Wisconsin.[1] The cause of their birth defects is not well understood, but scientists are taking their appearance as an urgent warning that something is seriously amiss in the environment.

For years, I have been interested in the ebb and flow of fraternal memberships in the United States.[2] I can state without fear of contradiction that fraternal membership is not now the social norm. All fraternal organizations suffered during the last half of the twentieth century; some declined to the point of virtual disintegration. It was while studying fraternal statistics in Maryland that I became aware of what may be a subtle warning sign for Freemasonry, perhaps a harbinger, like the deformed frogs of Minnesota and Wisconsin.

I have been interested in explaining the different fortunes of the York and Scottish Rites in this century. In 1900, there were 839,000 Freemasons in the United States; Royal Arch Masons accounted for 27% and only 5% were in the Scottish Rite. By 1995, there were 2,153,000 Freemasons, but by then, 37% were in the Scottish Rite and only 15% were in the Royal

---

1   William Souder, "Hundreds of Deformed Frogs Pose Environmental Warning," *Washington Post,* Sep. 30, 1996, A1.

2   S. Brent Morris, "Trends Affecting American Freemasonry," *The Philalethes* 35, no. 2 (Apr. 1982): 16–17; "The Public Image of Freemasonry," *The Royal Arch Mason Magazine* 14, no. 4 (Winter 1982): 105–11; "The Siren Song of Solicitation," *The Royal Arch Mason Magazine* 14, no. 6 (Summer 1982): 163–68; "Boom to Bust in the Twentieth Century," *Transactions of the Texas Lodge of Research* 23 (1987–1988): 142–63.

Arch. The relative strength of the York Rite has declined from 27% to 15%, while that of the Scottish Rite has risen from 5% to 37%. This is a significant realignment of American Masonic activity!

This relative decline in fortunes between the York and Scottish Rites can be explained in various ways. The Scottish Rite is largely found in urban areas, and their dramatic increase in membership coincides with the rural-to-urban migration of the American population. The York Rite offers only one route to significant recognition: presiding over a local body. While no Masonic body could serve as a model of organizational efficiency, the Scottish Rite has a more stable governing structure with long-serving state leaders who can institute and support consistent policies and goals. It has recently been suggested that the theatrical staging of Scottish Rite degrees so appealed to turn-of-the-century Masons, that it "eliminated the competition."[3]

As interesting as these speculations are, they are not as intriguing as another discovery I made as I studied fraternal membership in Maryland for the twenty-five year period from 1970 to 1995. In 1970, Maryland had 46,000 Masons, and by 1995 they had declined 42% to 26,900. By comparison, Maryland Odd Fellows declined 63% from 2,610 to 971. Royal Arch membership declined 49% to 3,600 and the Scottish Rite declined only 5% to 8,794. These figures tell an interesting story about fraternalism in Maryland, but are part of a larger national trend of declining memberships in the United States. Odd Fellowship has been declining since about 1950, the York Rite since 1957, Freemasonry since 1959, and the Scottish Rite since 1978.

As I was doing my analysis, I decided to tally the new Masonic groups started in Maryland during the period from 1970 to 1995. My informal research, which probably overlooked several bodies, turned up the following new Masonic organizations in the state, and I doubt that Maryland is significantly different from other states.

At least twenty-one new Masonic organizations were started during the twenty-five year period of 1970 to 1995. One of these groups was a regular Lodge, one was a Council of Cryptic Masons, and one was a Scottish Rite Valley. The other seventeen that I counted were associated Masonic groups at the fringe of Masonry. While the general adult male population

---

3   C. Lance Brockman, "Catalyst for Change: Intersection of the Theater and the Scottish Rite," *Heredom* 3 (1994): 121–46.

in Maryland has little interest in the Craft, as witnessed by our declining membership, Maryland Masons themselves are enthusiastic. Almost once a year they form a new Masonic body in the state. Maryland Masons are so zealous about Masonry that they seem to be constantly looking for more ways to enjoy the mystic bonds of fraternal fellowship, even as our grand lodge membership continues its slow, sad decline.

Ancient, Free & Accepted Masons
- Bayside Lodge
- John R. Coats Memorial Lodge
- Daylight Lodge
- David Kerr Memorial Lodge

Philalethes Society
- Southern Maryland Chapter

Md. Masonic Research Society

Ancient & Accepted Scottish Rite
- Southern Maryland Valley

Scottish Rite Clubs
- Chesapeake Club
- Conowingo Club
- Carroll Club

Societas Rosicruciana in Civitatibus Foederatis
- Maryland College

Royal & Select Masters
- Acacia No. 24

Allied Masonic Degrees
- Old Line Council No. 234
- Southern Cross Council No. 268
- Chesapeake Bay Council No. 278
- Freestate Council No. 308
- Eastern Shore Council No. 301
- Tide Water Council No. 334

Royal Ark Mariners
  • Pride of Baltimore Lodge

Knight Masons of America
  • Baltimore Council

York Rite College of North America
  • Maryland College

New City Square Club

New Maryland Masonic Bodies: 1970–1995

But Maryland Masons have no apparent interest in forming new lodges or York Rite bodies. The list of new Maryland Masonic bodies speaks clearly to that. They love Masonic fellowship, but have no use for new lodges, the fundamental unit, the heart and soul of Masonry. And this is the interesting warning sign I alluded to earlier. Our most enthusiastic supporters—our active Masters Masons—are voting with their feet and quietly moving their Masonic activities to almost anything other than the basic lodge.

> In 1891 a young man moved to Chicago from Philadelphia. He began work as a soap salesman offering merchants baking powder as a premium for buying his soap. He noted that the merchants were more interested in the baking powder than the soap, so in 1892 he started selling baking powder and offered two packs of chewing gum as a premium. Once again his customers were more interested in his premium than his product, so in 1893 William Wrigley, Jr., a successful businessman who gave his customers what they wanted, went into the chewing gum business. The rest is history.[4]

The thoughtful Mason must wonder why so much Masonic energy is being expended away from the lodge. York Rite Masons in particular must wonder why we can't find candidates or officers, and yet these new Maryland groups, most of which draw their memberships exclusively from active York Rite Masons, are growing. It could be that these growing bodies require a simpler "infrastructure"—regalia, annual returns, and ritual proficiency—and are thus easier to start up and maintain. It could be that they are perceived as more prestigious and exclusive than lodges or chapters

---

4 Wm. Wrigley, Jr. Co., www.wrigley.com.

or commanderies. Most of these groups formed in Maryland are "invitational" bodies that recognize some service to Masonry. Who doesn't like to be recognized for hard work? Who doesn't like to belong to an exclusive group, membership in which is recognized and admired? And yet why can't we generate that sense of exclusivity and recognition in a lodge?

If I were smart enough to know the answers to the questions I have raised, I would sell the solution to each fraternal lodge in the country and become fabulously wealthy. In fact, we may be the wrong people to be asking the questions: we enjoy the status quo and revel in the current structure, otherwise we wouldn't be participating so enthusiastically (or reading essays like this one).

I would like to propose a possible answer:

TRADITIONAL MASONIC BODIES ARE OVERBURDENED WITH CONSTRICTING RULES AND NITPICKING REGULATIONS.

We suffer from short-tenured leaders who are given almost limitless power and no time to use it effectively. Grand lodges and grand York Rite bodies have little managerial continuity. Most grand lodges elect a new grand master each year; he barely has time to pick a motto and a flower before he's running around the state on the grand visitation circuit. He may start a new program or institute a new policy, but it will fade as fast as his flower without the wholehearted support of his successors, who may have their own hobbyhorses to ride. Only the Scottish Rite, with its long-serving state leaders, has created a managerial structure in Masonry that allows organizational continuity of significant programs and policies, rather than the mindless maintenance of the status quo.

Most Masonic bodies have a massively centralized authority, greater than that found in almost any other voluntary associations. Masonic presiding officers, both by tradition and by regulation, have extreme discretion in administering their enormous powers. Grand lodges have this centralized authority, an executive officer who can rule by decree, and a network of district deputy grand officers to enforce their rules and regulations. None of this makes it fun for local bodies. By contrast, the allied Masonic bodies that show growth lack a network to enforce the central authority. Their local groups are largely autonomous and have wide discretion in conducting their affairs. This freedom from central interference may be what is more appealing about an A.M.D. Council than a Symbolic Lodge. These allied

Masonic bodies are "lean and mean"—small organizations that can be flexible and quickly respond to their members' needs.

Grand lodges today are multi-million dollar operations, but they lack the managerial and organizational continuity they need to thrive. The foremost management theory today holds that decision-making and authority should be delegated to the lowest possible level where local managers best understand the immediate needs of the organization. What if we elected grand masters to five year or longer terms? What if a grand master could start a program, nurture it, and see it established and accepted in his jurisdiction? What if lodges were given the flexibility and responsibility to make decisions for themselves? And what if Masons were encouraged and rewarded to form and participate in new lodges?

Masonry is declining in membership, as are nearly all other voluntary associations.[5] Our members continue to be enthusiastic about the Masonic experience, just not in lodges. There is hope for the Craft if we can focus our members' enthusiasm back at the main body of Masonry, but this will require difficult changes. Some of the most urgent changes are administrative, but they strike at the heart of our Masonic culture as it has evolved over centuries. Our basic rewards structure is predicated upon presiding, and no one wants to reduce rewards. There is no reason why Masonry cannot use accepted management techniques nor is there any reason why control cannot be returned to local lodges. If we are not willing to put changes to a vote in our grand lodges, then our members will continue to vote with their feet and to move their Masonic energies to more rewarding activities. And if we could conduct post-election polls, we'd probably find a lot of these voters saying, "I love Masonry. It's Grand Lodges I can't stand."

First published: "Transactions," *Texas Lodge of Research* 33 (2000)

---

5   Robert D. Putnam, *Bowling Alone* (New York: Simon & Schuster, 2000).

A Silver Lining in the Clouds

*Despite Continuing Membership Losses, Changes
Today Can Lead to a Stable Fraternity Tomorrow*

The winds and the waves are on the side of the ablest navigator.

—Edward Gibbon

Membership in American Blue Lodges peaked in 1959, at about 4,103,000, followed by over 40 years of decline to about 1,800,000 in 2002. The Scottish Rite (Northern and Southern Jurisdictions combined) has had 21 years of falling numbers since cresting in 1979 at 661,000. These numbers are a source of objective curiosity—*Why did this happen?*—and subjective dismay—*What will happen to us!* Knowing where we are and where we might go will help us plan for the future.

The average member in the Southern Jurisdiction in 2001 was 66.3 years old; 25% were under age 57, and 25% were over age 77. If our members had joined at a steady rate over the years (with no disruptions from military or economic crises), then there were fewer than expected for ages 56 to 71 and more than expected over age 71. Our 71+-year-old members are the strength and support of our fraternity, the brothers who grew the Scottish Rite to where it is today.

The average age of our 4,883 initiates in 2001 was 48.9, with 25% below age 38 and 25% above age 59. A good planner realizes at this point that there is almost a full generation between our initiates and our membership. This means that thoughtful efforts must be made to include plenty of new members in planning events for Valleys, or else we run the risk of creating a "generation gap" between our new members and valley activities. This is good advice in general: include a good sample of your members when planning any event—new and veteran, near and far, young and old, and so on.

The basic relationship of American Masonic bodies changed in July 2000 when the Shrine dropped the requirement that its members belong to either the Scottish or York Rites. During the five-year period 1995–1999, the Scottish Rite Southern Jurisdiction (S.J.) suffered an average net annual loss of 3.27%, the Northern Masonic Jurisdiction (N.M.J.) 3.20%, and the

Shrine 3.6%. In 2001 the S.J. lost 5.4%, the N.M.J. 5.0%, and the Shrine 3.3%. The bottom line: all Masonic bodies continue to lose membership. There is no quick fix.

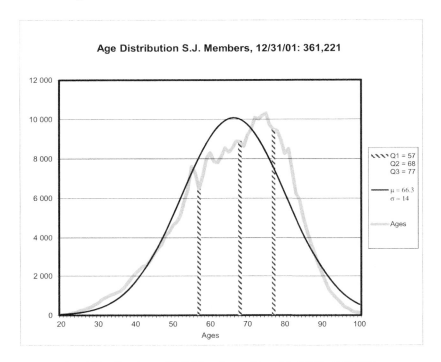

Age Distribution of S.J. Members, Dec. 31, 2001: 361,221

Brother John Belton has a simple formula to approximate Masonic membership:[1]

This Year = Last Year + Initiation + Affiliation
- Attrition - Deaths

In his formula, Attrition can be either a Demit or Suspension for Non-Payment of Dues (SNPD), and Affiliation includes Reinstatement. In the five-year period, 1995–1999, prior to the Shrine change, S.J. Attrition was 3.32 per 100 members or 3.32%, Initiation was 2.19%, Affiliation was 0.88%, and Death was 3.02%. If we continue at this rate, the S.J. will lose about 30% of its present membership by 2011.

---

1   John Belton, "Masonic Membership Myths Debunked," *Heredom* 9 (2001): 9–31.

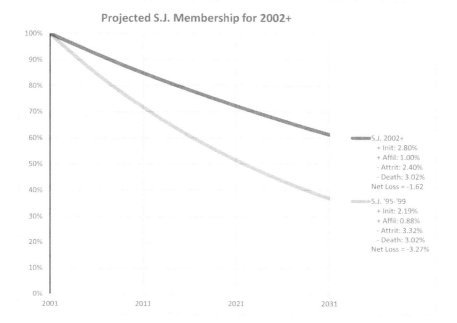

Projected Membership for S.J.: 2002+

Small changes, however, can have a dramatic effect on long-term trends. We can't do much about death rates, but we can aggressively work on Initiation, Attrition, and Affiliation. If we increase our initiation rate to 2.8 per 100 (increasing the 1995-1999 rate by a little over 25%), increase Affiliations to 1%, and decrease Attrition to 2.5%, then our losses in 2011 are only 15%, and our membership will decline at a slower more manageable rate. Given our large number of veteran members, loss is inevitable—but it does not need to be fatal.

A plan to achieve a smaller—but more effective—organization needs to focus on three essential points.

- Reduce Attrition with an aggressive dues collection program that includes personal contact with every member, not just those approaching SNPD.

- Meet the needs of current members by providing exciting activities and programs attuned to their interests and those of their families.

- Attract new members by being present and active in Blue Lodges and by providing fraternal and family activities that appeal to potential members.

There are winds and waves facing the Scottish Rite as we enter the twenty-first century. However, we are blessed with able navigators who have the vision to pilot us to even greater future successes.

The Public Image of Freemasonry
A Survey of the Literature Describing American Freemasonry

I don't know that much about the Masons, but they sure make good jars.

Freemasons have many reasons for being interested in their public image. At a very basic, almost egotistical level we would like to think that the community admires us for our membership. Everyone likes to take pride in what they do and in the groups they belong to, and Freemasons are no exception. On a more involved organizational level, our outward appearance is directly responsible for our lifeblood—the initiation of new Masons. Unbiased by friends and uninfluenced by mercenary motives, a candidate freely and voluntarily presents himself for the mysteries of Freemasonry. He should be prompted to solicit the privileges of Masonry by a favorable opinion conceived of the Institution—our public image.

Several approaches can be taken in examining our public image. Ideally, we'd like to carefully interview a large cross-section of the population, and determine their feelings towards religion, politics, education, civic duty, organizations in general, and Freemasonry in particular. This method is both expensive and time-consuming, and no Masonic organizations are yet interested enough in our image to support or fund such a study of the public. In fact, we're not even particularly interested in knowing about our own members. M.W. Brother Daniel C. Jenkins, Grand Master of Ohio, recognized this twenty years ago at the 1962 Conference of Grand Masters, observing, "one of our weaknesses … is our failure to analyze our membership by occupation, by talents, by education, and professional achievement."[1] We are then left with what few examples of recorded public opinion that can be found, anecdotes, written reports on Freemasonry, and findings of other researchers. The ultimate goal of this paper is to duplicate the conclusions of an intelligent researcher who knows nothing about Freemasonry, but who wants to know what people think about it.

There are occasional opportunities for a researcher to examine the popular opinions about Freemasonry, but they are so few that they can almost be ignored. Brother Dennis Treece reported in *The Philalethes* magazine about a radio talk show out of San Francisco that was devoted to Masonry.[13] The host invited Masons to call in to tell him about the Craft and particularly about its "secrets." I can only hope that few listeners tuned in, because the image presented was confusing at best.

Before describing the callers' responses, it is worth commenting on the host's conception of Freemasonry as a secret society. Now I know that it is an article of faith among Masons that ours is not a secret society, but a society with secrets. However, despite our continual pontifications, Webster's definition of a secret society applies to Freemasonry (as well as to Odd Fellowship and to the Elks and to others): "Secret Society—any of various oath-bound societies often devoted to brotherhood, moral discipline, and mutual assistance." We must accept that a real part of our image is secrecy.

The callers to the talk show ran the gamut from sincere supporters to rabid detractors. Their common trait was an ignorance of Freemasonry, whether shown in a discussion of the profound importance of the 32° or in a failure to appreciate that there is no uniform Masonic law in the United States or in a solemn debate on whether Freemasonry dates from King Solomon or the Garden of Eden. "The whole affair must have left everyone with the same impression: that Masons seem to know only a little more than anybody else about Freemasonry, and even they can't agree on much."[13]

The only case of a direct survey of the public that I am aware of is a Louis Harris Poll, commissioned by the Imperial Council of the Shrine on attitudes towards the Shrine and knowledge of burn prevention.[7] While this was not a study of Freemasonry itself but of a major subdivision, it nonetheless gives us some important information and lets us make some inferences. The poll found that 90% of those contacted have heard of the Lions; 87% of the Shriners; 84% of the Masons and the Rotary; and 83% of the Kiwanis. Of those who had heard of the Shriners, 55% agreed that they operated hospitals. This means that only 48% of adult Americans have heard of Shriners' Hospitals. Considering the much higher visibility of the Shrine with their parades, circuses, public service advertising, and so on, we may conclude that most Masonic charities have even less recognition. To support this conclusion, I can add that in seven years in Maryland, I've met only one person who knew of Bonnie Blink, the Maryland Masonic home.

The visibility of the Shriners and their connection with community service has earned them a generally good image: 75% of those sampled hold favorable opinions about the Shrine, 2% hold unfavorable opinions, and 23% have no opinion. Most of the unfavorable opinions are due to the perception that the Shrine is a discriminatory organization. Finally, 41% of the people agree that Shriners are Masons, and 34% agree that they're "secretive." There is a large public awareness of the Shriners, but little accurate information. It may be inferred that Freemasonry, with its broader activities and much less flamboyant affairs, is subject to greater misunderstandings than the Shrine. Having exhausted these few direct sources, our researcher must now find some other method to measure public opinion about Freemasonry.

Of the research methods available, anecdotal reports are the least trustworthy, unless in large numbers. Not only are such accounts unreliable, but they can also lead to apparent contradictions. As an illustration of this, let me give you two brief examples. I worked with a fellow a few years ago whose cousin had received extensive orthopedic treatment at a Shrine Hospital. My colleague would sing the praises of the Shrine at the drop of a hat, and yet he had absolutely no interest in joining a lodge. On the other hand, my very first exposure to Freemasonry after moving to Maryland produced a different image of the Shrine for me. I was taken aside and told just exactly which Temple blackballed "those people" and which other Temple had been taken over by "them." While my enthusiasm for the Shrine in Maryland was cooled, my zeal for Freemasonry is unabated. With little effort, we can find dozens of other anecdotes—all interesting, perhaps amusing, but not very enlightening. For that reason, we'll move on to some other research method.

It is appealing to look to press reports of the Craft to determine our external appearance, but the appeal is shallow. Certainly we don't want to measure our public image by pictures of new officers nor by presentations of fifty-year pins nor by announcements of ham and oyster suppers. We would hope that journalism offers a medium in which an accurate picture of Freemasonry can be had, but this isn't always so. The American press rarely knowingly publishes false information, but by emphasizing only one facet of a complex story they can produce amazing distortions, both good and bad. Everyone has his favorite examples, and I'll share two of mine with you.

When I was Master of Patmos Lodge in Ellicott City, Maryland, the *Howard County Times* used one-third of their front page to describe the lodge and our 157th birthday. Through an innocent misconception, the reporter stated that 200 Masons in tuxedos attended Patmos Lodge every meeting night, and had done this for over 150 years!

At the other end of the spectrum is the instance of the Rainbow Girls in Iowa a few years ago. An Assembly there had elected a local girl to membership, but was then told by the Supreme Assembly that she could not be a member because her mother was African-American. The furor over this racist and unmasonic act against a twelve-year-old girl made national news when it was reported by the wire services. What didn't receive equal coverage was the almost immediate edict by the Grand Master of Iowa. He stated that the Supreme Assembly could either change its racist policies, or all Iowa Masons and lodges would be forbidden contact with the Order of Rainbow.

Neither of these examples presents accurate images of the Craft, but they are representative of what the press considers "news." We can console ourselves with the thought that most readers remember little of what they read, and then for only relatively short periods. The good as well as the bad images are lost in a fading blur of poor memories.

What then is our hypothetical researcher to do? Surveys of the public have not been made, anecdotes are unreliable, and news coverage tends to emphasize the extremes or the utterly trivial. Perhaps resorting to encyclopedias or published declarations of principles will yield greater insight. This method, though, can trap the unwary.

Consider the case of the Independent Order of Odd Fellows. To an uninformed observer, it is virtually indistinguishable from Freemasonry. Both orders have centuries-old traditions from England. Each maintains orphanages and retirement homes. Both have appendant orders for the zealous, the convivial, and the family (though Freemasonry has more). The governments of both orders are similar, with local lodges and state grand lodges (though Odd Fellowship has a national Sovereign Grand Lodge, which controls Grand Lodges and nearly all appendant bodies). Finally, the principles of "Friendship, Love, and Truth" differ from "Brotherly Love, Relief, and Truth" more in wording than in meaning. Our researcher would be hard pressed to distinguish materially between the orders on the basis either of their organization or of their laudable purposes.

However, Freemasonry has grown by 35% since 1920 and Odd Fellowship has dwindled by 90%![9] Our rather recent complaints of a 1% national attrition per year for the last two decades pale beside the Odd Fellows' staggering decline of 90% in 60 years. This frightening hemorrhage of the Odd Fellows' membership can only be described as the dissolution of this noble order as it once existed. Clearly then, knowledge either of external organization or of platitudinous principles gives no deep insight into a society.

A possibly better source of information is Masonic publications. By considering those subjects that receive consistent and wide coverage, we may get a better glimpse of the image we want to project. In this analysis, the Grand Chapter of Maryland must appear rather silly: we're not willing to assess ourselves $0.50 per issue to deliver the quarterly *Royal Arch Mason Magazine* to our Companions. The Knights Templar come through for the York Rite, however, and send their fine magazine to all Sir Knights. The *Free State Freemason* will not yield much in this type of study, though, as it is essentially a "house organ," devoted primarily to telling what has been or what will be happening.

Pamela Jolicoeur and Louis Knowles, in an article in the *Review of Religious Research,* studied the Scottish Rite by this method.[5] The dominant theme they found in the literature was that of raising "the level of understanding of the citizenry concerning the mythology of America, its origins and its enemies." Almost 20% of the articles they sampled mentioned the American Constitution. One of the major issues they saw was a staunch defense of the Constitution and the identification of it as inspired by Masonic thought. This certainly goes enthusiastically beyond the Second Charge of Anderson's *Constitutions* of 1723: "A Mason is a peaceable Subject to the civil power...."

Unfaltering support for Americanism may be an image we want to project, but only those who read our publications see it. Again we find another avenue of research unproductive (this time because our writings get such little public exposure). This leads me to what I consider to be the only meaningful measure of our public image: a description of the men who are Freemasons. At the 1966 Conference of Grand Masters, M.W. Brother Alexander Duff, Grand Master of Manitoba, said, "The profane world has no criteria by which to judge Freemasonry other than by the fruits produced by the Masonic lives of those who are members of our beloved Craft."[2]

There may be few polls of popular opinion towards Freemasonry, but fortunately for our researcher there are several important studies of Freemasons; we will refer principally to three. The first is a survey of Texas Masons made in 1978 by the Committee on Printing of the Grand Lodge of Texas.[8] It is flawed because it overemphasizes the responses of officers and of active Masons, and thus does not reflect the Craft as a whole. Next is the 1975 Master's thesis on geography of Brother Burton A. Kessler, which looks at characteristics of the Illinois counties that had large numbers of Masons in 1970. Finally, there is the detailed 1977 Grand Lodge survey of Kansas Masons conducted by Professor John Wilson of Duke University and Brother S. Brent Morris.[10,14] While this latter study is the most far reaching and important, it too is flawed. Financial and organizational problems kept the return rate of the questionnaires at 37%. This means that some of their conclusions are only tentative.

Before dealing with this data, our theoretical researcher should consider one other factor: how well do studies in Illinois, Kansas, and Texas describe the Craft in Maryland? Certainly we don't expect those reports to be as accurate a reflection of Maryland Masonry as an analysis of Delaware or New Jersey would be, but then the latter surveys have never been made. We'll do the best we can with what we have, keeping in mind that Masonry in the Midwest may differ somewhat from Masonry in Maryland.

Sixty percent of the Masons sampled in Kansas were over 50, as compared to 35% of the general population in Kansas. This characteristic of age is supported by the Illinois study, and is probably explained by two factors. First, as suggested by the Louis Harris poll, Freemasonry usually attracts men who are well settled in their communities, and are thus older. Second, as Wilson noted, Freemasonry generates a more intense loyalty than voluntary associations in general, and tends to retain its members for life. This lifelong loyalty is seen in the 62% of the Kansas respondents who had been Masons 20 years or more.

Masonry in Illinois, Kansas, and Texas is rural, with the Texas and Kansas studies showing that 46% and 20% of the Masons, respectively, live in towns of less than 5,000. This trend, however, is not seen in Maryland. The 1980 US Census shows that less than 30% of the potential Masonic population lives in Baltimore City and County, but about 50% of Maryland Masons are from there. Masonry in Maryland, then, is more strongly urban than rural.

In Kansas and Texas, education and income figures for the Craft are nearly the same: less than 10% of the members had only an elementary education and over 50% had a college education; about 40% made from $10,000 to $20,000 per year and about 40% made over $20,000. Freemasons are thus much better educated and (allowing for the lower retirement income of many of our older members) wealthier than the population at large. In addition to the esteem associated with wealth and education, Kansas Masons were more than twice as likely to have a professional or managerial occupation than other citizens. However, there are signs of a declining socioeconomic status: adjusting for age factors, "Masons who joined prior to 1955 were 33% more likely to have managerial or professional jobs and 19% more likely to have obtained a college degree."[14]

In Iowa in 1958, the average age at Initiation was 35, and in Wisconsin in 1957 it was 40.[3,4] Empirical evidence suggests that the age is lower in Maryland now. The Texas results showed that 42% of those questioned (who by design were mostly active Masons) had been in the Craft 5–10 years. This was confirmed in the Kansas survey, where Wilson noted that "it seems as if, whatever the age of joining, becoming a member is followed by a flurry of activity which subsides over time."[14]

Before concluding our research of the literature describing Freemasons, there are a few remaining facts that bear noting. They don't really help with our profile, but they are too interesting not to repeat. The Texas report found that the more active a man was in Masonry, the less likely his sons were to join. Perhaps the sons are dissuaded by the many nights they see their fathers spend away from home and family? Still from Texas, 7% of Masons' sons were in De-Molay, 26% of their daughters were in Rainbow, and 51% of their brothers were in Masonry. In Kansas, 12% of the Masons had been DeMolays, and 36% of their fathers had been Masons. Kansas Masons are rather inactive in collateral bodies: 48% belonged to none and 40% belonged to only one or two.

By this point, our hypothetical researcher is probably exhausted, but he now has the data before him to prepare his summary. Freemasonry is widely recognized and respected in the community, especially by older, well-established residents. Most people are aware of its reputation for mutual assistance and somewhat less aware of its philanthropy (and this awareness probably comes from associating Masonry with the Shriners). Rightly or wrongly, the Craft is seen as a secret society with vaguely discriminatory membership policies. Many people wrongly assume, at the least, that Catholics are barred from membership, if not that Masonry is actively anti-Catholic. Virtually none of the citizenry understands the government of Freemasonry, and most attach outlandish importance to the 32° (and particularly the 33°) of the Scottish Rite. There is a small but dogged group in the public (and in the Craft) that associates Freemasonry with occultism and mysticism.

Freemasons tend to be older, wealthier, and better educated than the population at large. Most new Masons are in their early thirties, and the majority of the active core is in their early to mid-forties. Members are more likely to have professional or managerial jobs, and they have a tenacious loyalty to the Craft. In Maryland, Baltimore City and County produce proportionately more Masons than the rest of the state. In a Mason's family, his brothers are as likely as not to belong to a lodge, but his father is not as likely to belong, and a Mason's sons are unlikely to be in DeMolay.

Freemasonry has always valued the virtues of silence and circumspection, and thus historically has maintained a low profile. By well-established and prudent custom, we do not participate in or sponsor the types of activities people now associate with fraternal orders and community clubs. These factors, plus the over half-century decline in fraternalism as an important part of American life, have produced a situation where the public simply no longer is conscious of us.[11,12] Despite these negative elements, Freemasonry is still well known and respected in the community. We may not be at the center of public attention, but we do have an enviable reputation and image we can take deep pride in.

REFERENCES

1. Conference of Grand Masters of Masons in North America. "What Can We Do as Masons to Give More Publicity to our Craft and Its Activities?" *Proceedings,* February 20–21, 1962, 114–28. Washington: Conference of Grand Masters, 1966.

2. ———. "What, if Anything, Can Be Done About the Lack of Interest in Masonry by Non-Masons?" *Proceedings,* Feb. 23–24, 1966, 85–103.

3. Delzell, Earl B. "Age and Occupational Statistics for Initiates of 1958 in Iowa." *Grand Lodge Bulletin, Grand Lodge of Iowa, A.F.&A.M.* 60, no. 5 (May 1959): 131–32.

4. Grossenbach, Paul W. "What are the Causes for the Continuing Decline in Masonic Membership and What Remedies Can Be Suggested to Stop the Trend?" *Grand Lodge Bulletin, Grand Lodge of Iowa, A.F.&A.M.* 60, no. 5 (May 1959): 133–37.

5. Jolicoeur, Pamela and Louis Knowles. "Fraternal Associations and Civil Religion: Scottish Rite Masonry." *Review of Religious Research* 20, no. 1 (1978): 3–22.

6. Kessler, Burton A. "Some Geographic Aspects of Freemasonry in Illinois, 1970." Master's Thesis, Western Illinois University, 1975.

7. Louis Harris and Associates, Inc. *A Study of Public Attitudes towards Shriners and the Shrine of North America and a Study of Family Knowledge and Behavior in Fire and Bum Prevention.* Study No. 804,004. New York: Louis Harris, 1980.

8. Masonic Service Association. *Crystal-Balling the Future, The Results of a 1978 Computer Survey of Texas Freemasonry.* Edited by Stewart M. L. Pollard. Silver Spring: M.S.A., 1979.

9. Morris, S. Brent. "A Fraternal Abstract of the United States: 1900–1980." Manuscript, Columbia, MD, 1981.

10. ——— and John Wilson. "A Survey of Kansas Freemasons, 1977." Manuscript, Duke University, 1978.

11. ———. "Trends Affecting American Freemasonry." [Maryland Masonic Research Society, February 6, 1982.] *The Philalethes* 35, no. 2 (April 1982): 16–17.

12. Schmidt, Alvin and Nicholas Babchuk. "Trends in U.S. Fraternal Associations in the Twentieth Century." *Voluntary Action Research: 1973.* Edited by David Horton. Lexington Books, 1973.

13. Treece, Dennis P. "More Light in Masonry. " *The Philalethes* 35, no. 2 (Apr. 1982): 18–19.

14. Wilson, John. "Voluntary Associations and Civil Religion: The Case of Freemasonry." *Review of Religious Research* 22, no. 2 (1980): 125–36.

Presented to The August Scene, Deep Creek Lake, Maryland, August 7, 1982

On Masonic Research

An Inaugural Address as President of the
Maryland Masonic Research Society

Masonic research is a topic that has fascinated me for years, and it gives me great pleasure to share some of my thoughts with you on the matter. Perhaps I should reconstruct, as best I can, my first encounter with Masonic "education." I petitioned Highland Park Lodge, No. 1150 in Dallas, Texas, on my twenty-first birthday, while a senior at Southern Methodist University. In my zeal for light in Masonry, I had read nearly every book on the Craft in the university library together with most of those in the Dallas public library. Little did I know that this already made me better read than most Masons in Texas.

After my election, my family and I were invited to the lodge for a brief orientation program. This consisted of a short history of Freemasonry, with emphasis on the Craft in Texas. Then the lodge expert on Masonry took the floor and solicited questions. Being young, eager, and excited, I took him at his word about questions.

I began my windup by noting that, "The Grand Lodge of Texas is styled 'A.F.&A.M.' while the Grand Lodge of New York, for example, is styled 'F.&A.M.'"

He nodded with pleasure that one of his audience had read a little about the fraternity. Then I, with all innocence, threw the curve ball—a question that had indeed puzzled me and that I thought indicated I had done my background reading, "Is this because we are descended from the Grand Lodge of Antients and New York is descended from the Grand Lodge of Moderns?"

His demeanor changed, a puzzled frown came over his face as he asked, "Antients? Moderns? I don't believe that I understand your question."

I followed through with, "You know, the two rival Grand Lodges in London created either by a schism or by disagreement over ritual and procedures."

By now he was visibly distressed, "Two Grand Lodges? In England?! And formed by a schism!"

I quickly stepped in, "Of course, they reunited in 1813."

"Well, I should hope so!" was his quick rejoinder. "Are there any other questions?"

Undaunted, I pressed on, "Why is it that there are no lodges of Royal Ark Mariners in the United States?"

His composure was quickly restored as he sensed that control had returned to him, "Son, you have not read much on Masonry. Why I myself belong to the Royal Arch, but we call our local bodies *chapters,* not *lodges.*" I knew I was lost for the moment, but I vowed to continue in my search for Masonic light.

Masonic research, when done well, is fascinating to nearly anyone, whether in doing the work or in enjoying the results of the labor. It reveals the history, the lore, and the personalities that have made Freemasonry what it is today. Masonic research can reveal much of hidden significance in history, literature, and politics, and while it has a nearly universal attraction, few Masons undertake quality research. They may be frightened by the prospect of the unknown (that is, engaging in original intellectual inquiry), unsure of their ability to commit their work to writing, or sidetracked too easily into trite, trivial, or simply false studies.

It is my intention to address the first and last mentioned stumbling blocks to sound Masonic research. The problem of writing almost solves itself if you are excited about your work and have done your research. Beyond referring to a good English composition textbook, my best advice is for you to consult with other well-read brethren for counsel. On the other topics though, I think that I can point out some of the major pitfalls to avoid, and, I hope, inspire you to set out on your own study of some interesting and significant topics.

To begin with, be leery of any research topic that takes you away from the United States during the nineteenth and twentieth centuries. Almost anything outside of this period will require your reliance on someone else's studies (and on their accuracy). Albert G. Mackey, for example, was as prolific as he was inaccurate. He had his own pet theories on Freemasonry, and adjusted his view of history to fit his preconceived notions. His list of Landmarks is a classic example of a fabrication foisted upon the Craft, a fabrication that many Grand Lodges now wear as albatrosses around their necks.

Papers of the general type "Why Masonry is a Wonderful Organization" may be touching, moving, and interesting, but they are not good, solid research. They express, often eloquently, the deeply held affections of Masons for the Craft, but they don't qualify as research. The classic trite article on Masonry is something along the lines of "George Washington and Other Great Americans who were Freemasons." Such a topic can be original and fascinating, but it is far too often a rehash of stale material.

Having now told you what not to do, it would hardly be fair for me to fail to offer some positive suggestions. The first step towards good research is to read—read history, literature, current events, and particularly Masonry. Visit the libraries in the Grand Lodge, in the Whitehurst lounge at the Scottish Rite Temple in Baltimore, at the House of the Temple, and at the George Washington National Masonic Memorial. Browse in used bookstores and in flea markets looking for Masonic volumes; be sure to consult the Enoch Pratt Library and the Maryland Historical Society. At all times, though, be leery of believing everything you read.

Whenever you read, keep alert to unanswered questions in your mind. In fact, the very first requirement for a good research topic is that it should intrigue you, for if you are not excited, then you can hardly hope to interest anyone else. If you are curious about more details after reading an article, then you probably are on the track of a good topic. Finally, be aware that not all research leads to a finished product; much of the thrill is in the chase, rather than the capture.

Now for some specific details. Consider the coat of arms of the Grand Lodge of Maryland: it is almost an exact copy of the coat of arms of the United Grand Lodge of England, reflecting the coats of arms of the Antients and of the Moderns. When did we adopt our coat of arms? Why did we copy the United Grand Lodge of England? Since the United Grand Lodge was not formed until 1813, and the Grand Lodge of Maryland was formed in 1787, did we have another coat of arms from 1787 to the adoption of our current armorial bearings?

Examine the jewels in your lodge, or in the Grand Lodge museum, or in any lodge for that matter, particularly an old set that may be gathering dust. If your lodge's jewels were clearly produced by modern manufacturing techniques, then there is probably little interest in them. However, if they have the look of being handmade by a craftsman or of being quite old, then they may have a good story to tell. Was the artisan a brother? Did the lodge order the jewels or were they a gift? While you're looking at jewels, dig out your Tiler's sword and see if it has a story to tell.

On the topic of jewels, consider the magnificent bejeweled square of the Grand Master of Masons in Maryland. Who made it? Who commissioned it? When was it made? What is its current value? Are there any occasions when it was lost or was part of an unusual experience?

If you belong to an older lodge, what happened to it during the Civil War? If you don't belong to a lodge that old, then check the records of extinct lodges in the Grand Lodge Archives or of extant lodges you're interested in. Did the lodge express any strong partisan sympathies? Were there any resignations or trials because of the strife? Did the members or officers serve in either the Federal or the Confederate forces? Were any unusual tales of wartime fraternalism recorded in the minutes? Did the local newspapers report any activities of the lodge or of its members?

A fascinating branch of history that has only recently received any scholarly recognition is oral history. This is the collective memory of an organization or of a people as preserved in stories and tales. For example, who hasn't heard of the handwritten copy of our ritual stored in the Grand Lodge archives and available only to the Grand Master? Perhaps your lodge has preserved through tales, repeated and retold through the years, similar interesting tidbits. Seek these out and look for the true story behind the legend.

Speaking of the Grand Lodge Archives, a few hours there can produce a wealth of material for research papers. For example, there is the Raffle Book, which lists in precise detail the expenses and profits of the hundreds and hundreds of lotteries held by the Grand Lodge to pay for the Grand Lodge Temple. There are the early record books with some of the correspondence of the period. In August 1831, you can read of the inquiry of Nathan B. Haswell, Grand Master of Vermont to Benjamin C. Howard, Grand Master of Maryland. Brother Haswell asked if the Grand Lodge of Maryland had considered dissolving because of the current anti-Masonic furor. Brother Howard responded with a spirited defense of Freemasonry, and you can see in later correspondence that his letter was influential in persuading the Grand Lodge of Vermont not to disband.

The difficult times during the anti-Masonic period should be a great source of research. Did your lodge survive from 1826 to 1840? What of the lodges that expired? What of the Anti-Masonic political party candidate for President, William Wirt of Baltimore? What did the newspapers of the day have to say on the excitement?

As a final source of topics, consider the Revolutionary War. It is beyond my self-imposed limit of the nineteenth century, but it could produce significant, original studies. Rather than taking the standard approach of looking for outstanding revolutionists, see if you can find any loyalist Masons from Maryland. What trials did they suffer? What became of them, of their families, and of their Masonic affiliation after the war?

Let me conclude my meanderings by sharing with you one last idea gleaned from reading *The Poetry of Freemasonry,* by Rob Morris. It is a brief poem entitled "The Death of the Grand Master."

The Death of the Grand Master
Rob Morris, Poet Laureate of Freemasonry

> His voice was low, his utterance choked,
>   He seemed like one in sorrow bound,
> As from the Orient he invoked
>   God's blessings on the Masons round.
>
> 'Tis sad to see the strong man weep—
>   Tears are for sorrows yet untried;
> But who with sympathy can keep,
>   When age unseals emotion's tide?
>
> Reverently stood the Brothers round,
>   While their Grand Master breathed farewell,
> And strove to catch the faintest sound
>   Of accents known and loved so well.
>
> He told them of the zealous care
>   Of their forefathers of the Art;
> How valley-gloom and mountain-air
>   Bore witness of the faithful heart.

He conned the precepts, line by line—
    On, that the Craft may ne'er despise
Precepts so precious, so divine,
    That shape the Mason mysteries!

He warned them of a world unkind,
    Harsh to the good, to evil mild,
Whose surest messengers are blind,
    Whose purest fountains are defiled.

He told them of a world to come,
    To which this life a portal is,
Where tired laborers go home,
    To scenes of never ending bliss.

Then of himself he humble spoke—
    So modestly! so tenderly!
While from the saddened group there broke
    An answering sigh of sympathy:

"Now give me rest; my years demand
    A holiday, Companions dear!
My days are drawing to an end,
    And I would for my end prepare.

"Now give me rest; but when you meet,
    Brothers, in this beloved spot,
My name upon your lips repeat,
    And never let it be forgot!

"Now unto God, the Mason's Friend,
    The God our emblems brightly tell,
Your dearest interests I commend—
    Brothers, dear Brothers, oh farewell!"

Down from the Orient, slowly down,
    Weeping, through that sad group he passed,
Turned once and gazed, and then was gone,
    That look—his tenderest and his last.

His last—for, ere the week had sped,
    That group, with sorrow unrepressed,
Gathered around their honored dead—
    Bore their Grand Master to his rest!

Now beyond the general touching story in the poem, why should we be particularly interested in this tale? Well, the Grand Master referred to is John Crawford, M.D., eighth Grand Master of Maryland. He served in the Grand East from 1801 to 1813. The event described occurred on May 3, 1813, and Most Worshipful Brother Crawford died on May 9, 1813. What did he accomplish during his term of office? Why was the Grand Lodge so moved by his death? How did he know that his end was near? There are many other questions, but I think that you can raise them yourselves.

My brethren, I hope that I have piqued your curiosity this evening and inspired you to do some digging on your own. There is no limit to what you can find, if you only keep in mind the important questions of any detective: "Who?"; "What?"; "Where?"; "When?"; "How?"; and, most importantly, "Why?"

Presented to Maryland Masonic Research Society, October 30, 1985

Masonic Toasts

In twentieth century America, loud, boisterous toasting and singing are virtually unknown at Masonic affairs. Their absence and our recent interpretation of temperance as abstinence are modern innovations to the body of Masonry. Indeed, an understanding of Freemasonry in its proper historical context demands a study of the Craft's early social customs, particularly those of drinking, toasting, singing, and banqueting.

By 1722, Freemasonry was a significant enough movement in London that it began to be parodied. An example of thasses

is poking fun at the Craft is the ribald, anonymous poem entitled "The Free Masons: An Hudibrastick Poem." In addition to a scandalously preposterous exposure of the "secrets" of Masonry, there was a rather lengthy discussion of Masons' toasting customs. We note that the drinking and toasting of the lodges must have been well known, otherwise it would not have been a good object of parody. This poem explains the Masons' favorite toast as follows:

> They drink, carouse, like any *Bacchus*
> And swallow strongest Wines that rack us;
> And then it is they lay Foundation
> Of Masonry, to build a nation.
> They various Healths strait put around,
> To ev'ry airy Female Sound;
> But *Sally* Dear's the Fav'rite Toast,
> Whose Health it is they drink the most. ... [1]

This refers, by the way, to Sally Salisbury, a noted woman of the evening. Apparently she and a gentleman had some sort of a disagreement, which resulted in Sally placing a knife in him, and the constabulary placing her in Newgate Prison.

When the Rev. James Anderson produced *The Constitutions of the Free-*

---

1   Douglas Knoop et al., *Early Masonic Pamphlets* (Manchester: Manchester University Press, 1945), 87.

masons in 1723, he included several songs then popular with the Craft. So important were singing and festivities to the fraternity, that the very first songster published in the United States was Brother Ben Franklin's 1734 reprint of Anderson's *Constitutions.* In Laurence Dermott's *Ahiman Rhezon* of 1754, which served as the Constitutions for the Grand Lodge of Ancients, songs of a rather humorous nature appeared. An example of such lighter fare is "The Mason's Daughter," which was reprinted in the United States in David Vinton's charming 1816 songbook, *The Masonick Minstrel.* This ditty tells the story of a Mason's daughter and her suitor, and in part says:

> None shall untie my virgin zone,
> But one to whom the secret's known,
>   Of fam'd freemasonry;
>
> In which the great and good combine,
> To raise, with generous design,
>   Man to felicity.
>
> This said, he bow'd, and went away:
> Apply'd—was made without delay;
>   Return'd to her again:
>
> The fair comply'd with his request,
> Connubial joys the couple blest
>   And long may they remain.[2]

Mildly salacious songs such as this, however, caused Masons to stand out in Puritan New England. Indeed, Masonic singing and toasting led to some of the earliest condemnations of the Craft. It is easy to imagine a blue-nosed critic sniffing his contempt: "Well you know those Masons-they actually sing songs after their meetings!" However, not all sentiments expressed in Masonic toasts and songs were risqué. A better sense of the Masonic spirit of these earlier times is given by the following "Toasts and Sentiments" from Vinton's *Masonick Minstrel.*

- The Brother who stands plumb to his principles, yet is level to his brethren.

- May ev'ry Mason RISE in the EAST, find refreshment in the SOUTH, and be so dismissed in the WEST, as to find admission into the *middle*

---

2 David Vinton. *The Masonick Minstrel* (Dedham. Mass.: Herman Mann & Co., 1816), 38–39.

chamber to receive the reward of a good man.

- The heart that conceals, and the tongue that never reveals.

- Love to ONE, friendship to a FEW, and good will to ALL.

- To HIM, who all things understood,
  To HIM, who furnished stone and wood,
  To HIM, who nobly spilt his blood—
      In doing of his duty;
  We hail the day! we hail the morn!
  On which those three great men were born!
  Who did the TEMPLE thus adorn
      With WISDOM, STRENGTH and BEAUTY.[3]

Since the turn of the century, our Grand Lodges have tried to eliminate the excesses of unbridled exuberance. We have seen the passage of gambling, drinking, toasting, and other ancient customs that offended the tender sensibilities of our brethren of the Victorian period; yet the essential spirit of fraternalism remains. We may be more somber today (and certainly more sober), but our enthusiasm for the Craft is undimmed (even if our mode of expression has been tamed). When we have the all too rare privilege of participating in the ancient custom of Masonic toasting, let us be enthusiastic, enjoy the spirit, and remember that we are continuing a tradition of good cheer and fun from our fraternity's very earliest days.

Presented to Albert Pike Lodge of Perfection,
Baltimore, Maryland, October 30, 1985

3   David Vinton, *The Masonick Minstrel*, 445.

Thomas H. Dyer: An Invisible Hero
A Biography of a Maryland Hero of World War II

Heroes, like people, are of many different types. There are ambitious heroes like Julius Caesar, noble heroes like Jacques DeMolay, and brave heroes like Horatio at the bridge. Their deeds are recounted, their exploits expanded, and their names enter the language as a sort of permanent memorial. In fact, the nearest thing to immortality on Earth is to have one's heroics remembered through the years.

Some heroes choose not to pursue the glory available to them after their deeds, but quietly try to return to their private lives. Marcus Cincinnatus, the Roman farmer-soldier, is an exemplar of the self-effacing hero. There is, however another type: the invisible hero. This is the person who acts beyond the call of duty, and then actively tries to remove any evidence of his participation. He has consciously chosen to receive no recognition, in the belief that this best serves the needs of his fellow men. Our Illustrious Brother, Captain Thomas H. Dyer, USN (Ret.), 33°, was such a hero.

Illustrious Brother Dyer spent most of World War II in a windowless basement office of the 14th Naval District's Administration Building in the Navy yard at Pearl Harbor. Heavy doors defended the room, locked gates were at the top and bottom of the stairs, and armed guards kept a careful watch. Captain Dyer headed the cryptanalysts of the Fleet Radio Unit, Pacific Fleet, and helped to produce the intelligence that led to American victory in the Pacific.

Admiral Isoroku Yamamoto, Commander in Chief of Japan's Combined Fleet sent a note to Prince Konoye before the war saying, "I must also tell you that, should the war be prolonged for two or three years, I have no confidence in our ultimate victory." Thus the Japanese strategy, as exemplified by the Pearl Harbor attack, was sudden surprise and rapid attack. If they could not quickly defeat the Americans, then US industrial strength would surely win a prolonged war.

Admiral Yamamoto planned a major naval attack on Midway, preceded by a diversionary attack on the Aleutians. The Japanese navy strongly outnumbered the American Navy with eleven battleships, five carriers, sixteen cruisers, and forty-nine destroyers to no battleships, three carriers, eight cruisers, and fourteen destroyers. Counting on surprise, the Japanese intended to force the over-extended American fleet to react to their advances, without any opportunity for coordinated defense. If the plan had been successful, Midway would have fallen and would have left Hawaii undefended. The strategy failed, and failed miserably because of Illustrious Brother Dyer and other invisible heroes in their basement office.

Well before the attack on Pearl Harbor, American cryptanalysts had broken the Japanese diplomatic code known as Purple and other Japanese codes. The extremely sensitive intelligence produced from this source was called Magic, and very likely saved thousands of American lives and shortened the war. Captain Dyer worked round-the-clock during the war, with his wife bringing him sandwiches in a picnic basket. He spent his hours decrypting and translating messages of the Japanese Combined Fleet.

The intelligence officers concluded in May 1942 that the Japanese were planning a major attack on Midway. Without revealing the invaluable success against the Japanese codes, Admiral Nimitz ordered the carriers *Hornet, Enterprise,* and *Yorktown* to a position that would be on Admiral Yamamoto's flank. On the morning of June 3, 1942, our planes attacked the Japanese carriers, and by the end of the day the carriers *Akagi, Kaga, Soryu,* and *Hiryu* were sunk. Admiral Yamamoto realized his defeat, cancelled the attack on Midway, and retreated. As a result of cryptanalysis, Army Chief of Staff, Brother and General George C. Marshall said, "We were able to concentrate our limited forces to meet their naval advance on Midway when otherwise, we would almost certainly have been 3,000 miles out of place."

Admiral Yamamoto had another and deadlier encounter with the intelligence produced by Illustrious Brother Dyer. Yamamoto was one of the military geniuses of World War II, and his men idolized him. In the spring of 1943, he scheduled a one-day morale and inspection tour of bases in the upper Solomon Islands. Yamamoto was noted for both his tactical skills and his compulsive punctuality. The schedule decrypted in Dyer's basement office not only gave a virtual minute-by-minute itinerary for the tour, but also a perfect opportunity for a surprise attack against the master of surprise himself.

Admiral Nimitz then faced a particularly difficult choice. He could attack Yamamoto, thereby revealing his knowledge of the secret itinerary and by inference our ability to read Japanese codes. Or he could let Yamamoto go and preserve our great intelligence advantage. The death of Yamamoto surely would demoralize the Japanese, and his replacement as Commander in Chief certainly would be less able to plan the war or to inspire the men. The loss of our cryptanalytic advantage would have been disastrous in the case of Midway, and might have had worse consequences later in the war.

The solution was to have a "routine" reconnaissance flight spot and shoot down the Japanese planes. The explanation could be easily swallowed: the Commander in Chief of Japan's Combined Fleet had succumbed to bad luck. The actors were given their parts, the stage was set, and the curtain came down for the last time on Admiral Yamamoto on April 18, 1943.

There may be other successes attributable to Captain Dyer, but if so, they are still carefully hidden away as he intended. When his work was finished, he quietly packed away his tools and covered any public evidence of his efforts. He realized the immense value of cryptology to our victory, and he knew that it might play an equally vital role in the future. Rather than endanger in the slightest our future defense by accepting the well-earned plaudits for the thousands upon thousands of lives he saved, Brother Dyer quietly joined the ranks of the invisible heroes. Even his wife and family knew nothing of his work.

After the war, American intelligence efforts were carefully scrutinized. Past Sovereign Grand Commander, Henry C. Clausen, 33°, led the investigation, and reported to the Joint Congressional Committee in 1945:

> I also think that the basic recommendation that can come from this committee is a very fine one if you make it that never again shall Magic, this information, be monopolized by one service or the other service, but have it distributed by one agency on an overall basis.[1]

The recommendation of Grand Commander Clausen and others led to the establishment of a central cryptologic organization for the United States— the National Security Agency.

Illustrious Brother Dyer worked at the National Security Agency (NSA) after the war until 1955, when he then retired from the Navy and taught mathematics at the University of Maryland until 1967. He was born in Osawatomie, Kansas, in 1903, and he became a Master Mason in Annapolis

Lodge No. 89, A.F.&A.M. in December 1923, just before graduation from the Naval Academy in 1924. He received the 4° through the 18° in Long Beach, California, and received the 19° through the 32° in 1946 in Washington, DC. Brother Dyer was invested with the rank and decoration of Knight Commander of the Court of Honour in 1951 and coroneted an Inspector General Honorary of the 33° in 1961. He served as Commander of Robert de Bruce Council of Kadosh in Washington in 1964. Brother Dyer died January 5, 1985, of cardiopulmonary arrest in Baltimore, Maryland. Funeral services were conducted at the Chapel of the Arlington Cemetery and interment was at Arlington Cemetery.

REFERENCES

1. Kahn, David. *The Codebreakers.* Toronto: The Macmillan Company, 1969. (This book was used extensively in the preparation of this article, even though explicitly referenced only once.)

2. Barnes, Bart. "T. H. Dyer, Unsung Hero of World War II, Dies." *The Washington Post,* Jan. 8, 1985.

First published: *The New Age Magazine* 93, no. 7 (July 1985)

The Hidden Secrets of A Master Mason

A Speculation on Unrecognized Operative Secrets in Modern Masonic Ritual

Notre origine est respectable,
Ne la chargeons d'aucune fable,
   C'est une nuit;
La raison murmure & s'assige,
Lorsqu'on masque, par le prestige,
   Le jour qui luit, Le jour qui luit.*

—Baron Louis Theodore Tschoudy

*Our origin is respectable, Do not burden it with any fable, It is night; Reason murmurs and is afflicted, When one masks with illusion, The shining day, The shining day.

M asonic authors have been known to abandon all reason in their reveries upon Masonic symbolism. Their flights of fancy have produced such ludicrous outrages as the theory that Freemasonry originated with Adam in the Garden of Eden, or perhaps in ancient Egypt, or possibly even in fabled Atlantis. The latter notion is especially appealing to these dreamers as there is no evidence of the existence of that legendary continent, and, more importantly, there is no evidence to contradict their hypotheses.

I am not from Missouri, but I firmly subscribe to that state's motto in regard to Masonic research: "Show me!" There is more than enough antiquity and honor connected with our Craft to make references to unfounded claims and fanciful digressions unnecessary (and downright embarrassing!). Nonetheless, such speculations have had a profound effect upon the history of the Craft.

For example, the myriad of what are called "high degrees" were inspired almost entirely by a single event: the oration of Chevalier Ramsey in 1737.[1]

---

1   This statement is an error. Chevalier Ramsay's *Oration* seems to have inspired the chi-

This noble brother supposed that Freemasonry had been kept hidden in the Holy Lands following the destruction of King Solomon's Temple, and that the Knights Templar had received these hidden secrets during the Crusades. Upon their return to Europe, so the theory goes, the Knights established and spread Freemasonry. As romantic as Ramsey's ideas were, they fall in the category of wishful thinking rather than in that of demonstrable fact.

Having torn down the efforts of Masonic "scholars" who speculate without fact, I am now about to embark upon my own course of speculation! However, I begin by admitting that my thoughts are without solid foundation, though they may appear to follow firm evidence. The hidden secrets that I propose to find are not philosophical or symbolic, but practical. Certainly we can discover hidden in our ritual the ultimate goal of man to be a constant striving for perfection and for the discovery of God Whether this culmination is in a four-ettered representation of God (*yod he vau he* (יהוה) or I.N.R.I., for example) or in explicit resurrection symbolism, it is nonetheless pervasive in Masonic ritual. My goal is to examine elements of Masonic ritual and symbolism and to try to deduce what may be some still hidden in our ritual. The best that I can say of my conclusions is that they are reasonable guesses and (I modestly think) interesting speculation.

Let's begin by considering just exactly what sort of secrets an apprentice could learn in a medieval freemasons' guild. These secrets were presumably "trade or technical secrets, relating, for example, to the designing of an arch, or to the way in which a stone should be laid so that its grain ran, so far as possible, as it did in its native bed in the rock."[6]

Also, we must not forget private means of recognition, which may have served then in place of a union card. During the sixteenth and seventeenth centuries in Scotland, it became necessary to have a means of excluding cowans (i.e., non-union or scab workers) from legitimate Mason's work, and so the Mason Word evolved. Manuscripts of the period have described this word variously as *mahabyn, maughbin,* or *matchpin*—all reminiscent of our modern usage.[2,7] These examples suggest what an apprentice might learn during his tenure, but, except for the Mason Word, are absent from our present ritual.

-----

valric "high degrees." Our best estimate is that the growth of high degrees began with the Master Mason Degree in 1725 followed by the Scots Masons in 1733 and evolved from there.

I had hoped that in our modern ceremonies there still might exist, in no matter how adulterated a form, a few fragments of some early secrets. But how could such early esoteric knowledge be identified? Well, I thought to look for some symbolism with a particularly artificial explanation. This might have resulted from Preston or some other ritual editor not only not wanting to discard an ancient emblem, but also not entirely understanding its significance, or maybe thinking it too well known to need elaboration. Perhaps I could find some portion of ritual logically detached from the ceremonies surrounding it. This also could be an ancient and forgotten usage that no one dared remove. Who knows, I might be able to deduce the ultimate operative secret, the *arcanum arcanorum*—long lost, now found, Holiness to the Lord!

As I considered this problem, it was significant to me as a mathematician that geometry and Masonry were so closely linked in our ritual. For example, in the Fellowcraft Degree, we learn that "the fifth science, geometry, is most revered by Masons." The statement that "geometry or Masonry [were] originally synonymous terms" seems to further support this connection. Two of the great lights of Masonry, the square and compasses, were instruments used by the classical geometricians from Euclid forward. The oldest known Masonic document, the *Regius Poem* of the second quarter of the fifteenth century, uses the term geometry to mean masonry and architecture. Finally, the Master of a Lodge, the one who in our operative period certainly possessed all of the secrets of the Craft, has as his emblem of office a square. These all seemed to point to some great significance of geometry, with perhaps the square symbolizing something particularly important.

With these clues before me, I needed only a final hint to draw my conclusions. The catalyst came from reading a reprint of the *Dumfries Manuscript No. 4*. This document is one of our Gothic constitutions, and dates from the late 1600s, during the period of transition from operative to speculative. Among other items in the manuscript, there is a discussion of a class of Masons known as "lewises" (apprentices who had not been admitted as Master Masons). Specifically, it laid down that a master or fellow "shall not make any mould, square or rule for any who is but a lewis."[6] Further study of these constitutions shows that the restriction against making molds, squares, and rules for non-Masons is a common feature. Examples can be found in the following manuscripts: the *Landsdowne* of about 1560; the

Grand Lodge of 1583, the *Buchanan* of the seventeenth century; and the *Antiquity* of 1686.[3, 4, 9, 13]

Thinking over these passages, I first wondered why anyone would care if a lewis had a square. Then it dawned on me—not everyone knows how to make a square! Four centuries ago, you just couldn't walk down to the local hardware store to buy one. It required a special "secret" to make a square, and further "secrets" to test one to be sure it was true. Then I made my flight of fancy: one of the original secrets of Masonry must have been the geometric skills needed to make and try a square!

With my hypothesis in hand, the hunt for evidence began in earnest. Certainly Freemasonry and geometry have been connected from our earliest periods, as seen in nearly all of the Gothic constitutions from 1390 on. The emblem of the Master could be interpreted as a constant reminder of his ability to make a true square. Then I recalled from the Fellowcraft degree that "a square is an angle of ninety degrees, or the one fourth part of a circle." I had always thought that this was a peculiar and rather non-meaningful statement. That is, until I reexamined it in light of my new hypothesis.

To anyone who has completed a normal high school course of study today, it is no surprise that a circle divided into four equal parts produces four right angles, or that an angle of 90° is the angle of a square. However, to the uneducated masses of several centuries ago, this might have been a significant revelation. Possibly it was one of the first things learned after an apprenticeship (much as it is today!).

There is, though, a more practical explanation. This could be a reminder of a "field test" for testing the trueness of a square. Here's how it is done. First, the square is placed on a flat surface so that the arms are at 12:00 and 3:00, and a line is drawn along the vertical arm. Then the square is flipped down so that the arms are at 3:00 and 6:00, and then it is flipped over so that the arms are at 6:00 and 9:00. Finally, it is flipped up so that the arms are at 9:00 and 12:00. If the square is true and the flipping has been careful, then the vertical arm should align with the line drawn in the first step. Even today, carpenters use this technique as a quick test of trueness (see Figure 1).

Searching through our symbolism for further clues, I next came to the familiar emblem of a point within a circle, which we are told "is represented in every regular and well governed Lodge...."[13] Why should every lodge contain this curious device? Perhaps there was more than just artificial symbolism attached? The veil was lifted when a friend, Brother Jerry E. Marsengill of Iowa, remarked that this could be used to try a square.

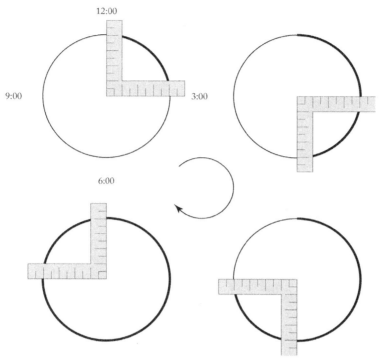

Figure 1. Trying a square by quartering a circle.

Of course! Every lodge of operative Masons had to have some way of testing the trueness of its instruments, especially a square, a method more refined than the simple circle quartering. The technique is easy, quick, and absolutely accurate (see Figure 2). First, a line is drawn through the center of the circle (the point) so that it intersects the circle on each side. Call these points of intersection A and B. Now the square is placed so that any point on one of its outside edges touches point A, and the other outside edge touches point B. If the square is true, its outside corner will just touch the circumference of the circle. This method of testing could be an invaluable "secret" of the medieval Freemason. In fact, it is simply Proposition 31 of Book III of Euclid's *Elements of Geometry* (Thale's Theorem): "In a circle, the angle in the semicircle is right. ..." (See Figure 3.)

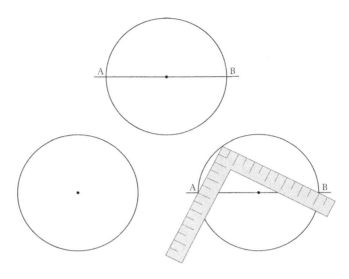

Figure 2. Trying a square with a point within a circle

The final piece of evidence is, I think, the most convincing: the Forty-seventh Problem of Euclid (actually Proposition 47 of book I of *The Elements*). One of the earliest pieces of officially sanctioned Masonic artwork is the frontispiece of Anderson's *Constitutions* of 1738, and there appears this ubiquitous Masonic device. The Grand Lodge of Pennsylvania, which traces its ancestry to the Grand Lodge of Antients in England, is said to have the oldest and least adulterated ritual in the world today. The Pennsylvanian emblem for a Past Master is a square over the forty-seventh problem. (See Figure 4.)

The significant point about the use of the forty-seventh problem is that when specific dimensions are shown, a 3-4-5 right triangle is most often depicted. That is, the two legs are of lengths 3 and 4 and the hypotenuse is of length 5. (See Figure 5.) This might be because the 3-4-5 triangle is the simplest example of the theorem, or it might be because this was the way operative masons made their squares! By taking three strings or rods, one each of lengths 3, 4, and 5, and putting them together to form a triangle, you will always have a right angle. Still today, foundations of buildings are laid out with strings in the 3-4-5 ratio. Again, we have a simple, effective, and essential "secret" of the operative builder.

As long as we are speculating, let's stretch things just a bit further, and make another tie-in to the forty-seventh problem. In "A Mason's Examination" of

1723, one of the early Masonic catechisms, there is an allusion to a curious Rule of Three: "If a Master Mason you would be. Observe you well the Rule of Three." Scholars have supposed that this refers to a method of giving the Mason Word in a "trible voice," possibly an early instance of Royal Arch ceremonies in Craft Lodges. However, we can imagine that this refers to the rule whereby the Masnter and Wardens of a lodge each take a staff (of lengths 3, 4, and 5) and put them together to make a right angle.[5]

With this view, the Hiramic Legend suddenly has an entirely new interpretation. Suppose that the only way our early Grand Masters knew to make a right angle was to put together their staffs, and they didn't understand the proportions required, only that their staffs had this "secret" property. If upon the death of Hiram Abif, his staff were lost, then indeed the Master's secret would be gone forever.[12] Solomon and Hiram of Tyre could never again hope to make new squares by this method—"Alas, poor Hiram!"

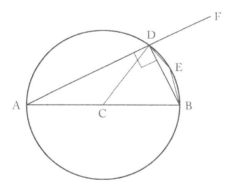

Figure 3. "In a Circle, the angle in the semicircle is right. ..."
Proposition 31, Book I, Euclid's *Elements*

Now the questions must arise. Is the ultimate secret of an operative master Mason the knowledge of how to make and try a square? Are there other, unrecognized secrets lurking in our ritual? Was medieval education such that these procedures would truly be startling revelations? Does a study of the evolution of our rituals support these hypotheses about the importance of making right angles? In answer to all of these questions, I must say: "I don't know." I promised a flight of fancy, not a carefully researched thesis. There haven't been any embarrassing cruises up the Nile in search of "Masonic Light," but bear in mind that the foundation of this mental exercise is just as unsteady as the sands of the Sahara. My personal opinion is that there is more than a grain of truth in these deductions. Let me remind you, however, that the best that can be said about these conclusions is that they are reasonable guesses and (I hope you will agree) interesting speculation.

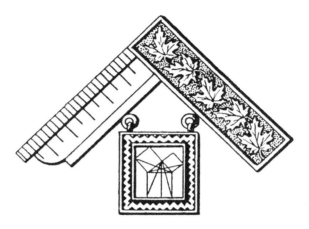

Figure 4. Pennsylvanian Past Master's emblem.
(From http://freemasonry.bcy.ca/ graphics.html. Used with permission.)

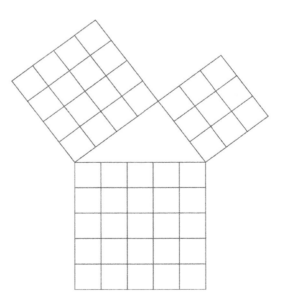

Figure 5. A 3-4-5 Triangle, the 47th Problem of Euclid,
or the Pythagorean Theorem.

Epilog

Brother William Burkle, 32°, has discovered an even better "hidden secret" for trying a square with the point within a circle. Start with the "standard" diagram and draw an arbitrary tangent line. The points of intersection with the two parallel lines and the center point of the circle form a right angle— and the "secret" tangent line that makes everything work can be erased after the test.

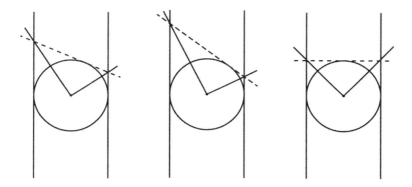

Figure 6. Burkle's method for trying a square with a point within a circle.

Burkle, William. "The Point Within a Circle—More than Just an Allusion?" *Scottish Rite Journal* (September-October 2007).

REFERENCES

1. Anderson, James. *Anderson's Constitutions of 1738.* Reprint. Blooming-ton, IL: Masonic Book Club, 1978.

2. Carr, Harry. *Six Hundred Years of Craft Ritual.* N.p.: Committee on Masonic Education, Grand Lodge of Missouri, 1977.

3. Coil, Henry Wilson. *Coil's Masonic Encyclopedia.* New York: Macoy Publishing and Masonic Supply Co., 1961.

4. Gould, Robert Freke et al. *The History of Freemasonry.* New York: John C. Yorston and Co., 1885.

5. Jones, Bernard E. *Freemasons' Guide and Compendium.* New York: Macoy Publishing and Masonic Supply Co., 1950.

6. Knoop, Douglas and G. P. Jones. *The Genesis of Freemasonry.* Manchester: Manchester University Press, 1949.

7. ———. *The Scottish Mason and the Mason Word.* Manchester: Manchester University Press, 1937.

8. ——— and Douglas Hamer. *The Early Masonic Catechisms.* Edited by Harry Carr. 2nd ed. London: Quatuor Coronati Lodge, 1975.

9. Mackey, Albert Gallatin and William R. Singleton. *The History of Freemasonry.* New York: Masonic History Co., 1906.

10. Roberts, Allen E. *The Craft and Its Symbols.* Richmond: Macoy Publishing and Masonic Supply Co., 1974.

11. Tschoudy, Baron Louis Theodore. *L'Etoile Flamboyante, ou La Société des Francs-Maçons Considérée sous tous les Aspects.* 1766. Reprint. Paris: Gutenberg Reprints, 1979.

12. Turnbull, Everett R. and Ray V. Denslow. *A History of Royal Arch Masonry.* 3 vols. Trenton, MO: General Grand Chapter Royal Arch Masons, 1956.

13. Webb, Thomas Smith. *The Freemason's Monitor.* Salem, MA: Cushing and Appleton, 1816.

———

Presented to Independent Royal Arch Lodge No. 2, F.&A.M.,
New York City, December 2, 1982

The Siren Song of Solicitation
The Case Against Easing Masonic Membership Practices

To the Sirens first shalt thou come, who bewitch all men, who-
soever shall come to them. Whoso draws nigh them unwittingly
and hears the sound of the Sirens' voice, never doth he see wife or
babes stand by him on his return, nor have they joy at his coming;
but the Sirens enchant him with their clear song.

—Circe to Odysseus, *The Odyssey*, Homer

Freemasonry has undergone many changes during the twentieth century, the most dramatic and troubling of which
are the changes in the size of our membership. From 1900 to
1930, we experienced constant growth and expansion, from
840,000 to 3,280,000 members (a 290% increase). The Depression and a changing social order took their toll as we lost
25% of our membership (from 3,280,000 to 2,460,000). Then
another spurt of growth brought two decades of increase, from
2,460,000 to 4,100,000 (up by two-thirds). Finally, from 1960
to 1980 we have endured a 21% decline to our current size of
3,250,000.[1] A cottage industry has been established among
the writers in the Craft devoted to analyzing, explaining, and
projecting these figures, and as yet no universally accepted
theory has resulted. The ultimate concern in all of these studies (and this present work included) is to ensure that our gentle Craft survives the recent attrition and returns to growth
and prosperity.

Most commentators are either rosily optimistic or depressingly somber in
their analyses. The Pollyannas, on the one hand, cheerily proclaim that no
institution founded upon principles as noble as ours can ever perish (and
then they carefully avert their eyes from the Odd Fellows, the Knights of
Pythias, and other withered orders). On the other hand, the Jeremiahs
gloomily project our losses and conclude that at most two more generations will know of us firsthand (and these doomsayers choose to ignore the

well-established cyclic nature of our membership and demographic trends in our population). What have been lacking most often are a calm study and a long-range analysis.

In recent years, some of our officials have given careful, thoughtful study to our latest declines and have sought to provide more than simple booster-ism as a solution. In Kansas on March 14, 1979, M.W. Brother W. Nolan Artz, Grand Master of Masons, waived restrictions on the time between degrees, on all proficiencies before advancement, and on the number of candidates per conferral. This was done for the explicit purpose of bringing in 5,000 petitions.[3] In Illinois in the same year, Grand Master Vance C. van Tassel granted an "amnesty" to all candidates who had allowed the time limit for their proficiencies to expire. These Illinois brethren were then permitted to advance without examination.[2] In Iowa and other jurisdictions, the "fellowship Night" is a popular way to introduce Freemasonry to prospective candidates. Illustrious Brother David O. Johnson, S.G.I.G. in Oregon, said, "Our attitude toward the non-solicitation of members is one of our greatest deterrents to membership increase." In each of these examples, however, our leaders have been lured by the siren song of solicitation: if it were only easier to get men into Masonry, our problems would be solved!

These brethren are to be praisedd for their courage in breaking with hidebound audition. M.W. Brother Bruce H. Hunt, P.G.M. of Missouri, said that "all this means that there are Grand Masters who are aware that something is wrong, and they are searching for a solution to the problem."[15] It is my opinion, however, that their solutions err in attacking the problem from the wrong end. There is nothing sacrosanct about the Masonic custom of rigid non-solicitation, but it is a custom we should be wary of tampering with.

Change is no stranger to Freemasonry, but it usually comes in small, nearly silent steps. We should not be afraid to consider alterations, but we should decide if they will produce merely procedural or truly fundamental changes. For example, removing the Volume of Sacred Law from our altars would leave us with an organization that would just no longer be Freemasonry. Then again, requiring each and every bill to be approved by a separate motion would lengthen our meetings, but would have little other effect. Somewhere between these examples of the ultimate and of the trivial lies the question of solicitation.

Certainly non-solicitation is not a landmark (not even Mackey included it in his silly list). It does indeed deter membership growth, but so do the requirements that petitioners believe in the Grand Architect, that they be educated enough to appreciate our ceremonies, and that they be able to pay our initiation fees. No one suggesting solicitation (or any of the other accelerations of the membership process) wants an indiscriminate flood of candidates. They only want a way to approach carefully selected potential Masons and to encourage them to seek our Light. Not only do I think that this approach is misguided, but I also think that it may divert our energies from other, more needed reforms.

In any discussion of solicitation, we must bear in mind that only "improper solicitation" is forbidden. Most American jurisdictions implicitly, if not explicitly, forbid any form of invitation, though many think it not improper to hold "Friendship Nights." W. Brother Harry Carr of England sums up the view that the British and I share on this sort of "non-solicitation." "The motives may be wholly praiseworthy, the proceedings and their environment may be completely dignified and respectable, yet, to our English way of thinking, this must surely be the most flagrant kind of 'improper solicitation.'"[1] Indeed, the determination of propriety is tricky, if not impossible.

With more than two centuries of a strict interpretation of "improper solicitation," it would be difficult, at best, for us to operate discreetly with even modest liberalization. Who has not seen, and been appalled by, the eager booster from some collateral body thrusting petitions into any and all unoccupied hands? Once we allow our members to proselytize, now soon before annual goals and quotas are set? How soon after this do we give awards to lodges showing the biggest increase or medals to the brother signing on the first line of the largest number of petitions? And when after this do we become indistinguishable from the service clubs, save in name and regalia?

"But," protest our radicals, "we want nothing of the sort! We want only a means to cautiously invite carefully screened candidates." In the words of Brother Johnson, "we would find men more concerned with the Order and more dedicated to service and attendance. It would tend to weed out the lukewarm and to strengthen our Organizations' basic structures."[6]

With these protestations, I most fraternally and firmly disagree. M.W. Brother Dwight L. Smith, Past Grand Master of Indiana, said it better than I ever could:

[anyone] who thinks a program of invitation could be controlled, discreet, dignified, so that only men of high caliber would be invited, is living in a fool's paradise. [What] reason do we have for thinking that our membership at large, representing all walks of life and all strata of society, would confine its efforts to the cream of the community?"[11]

We have too many lodges with failing memberships that would desperately latch upon this sort of plan as a short-term solution to long-term, fundamental problems (problems that they don't want to face).

Such a change in our membership procedures has no particular guarantee of working. Now the dissensions should start: "But look at service clubs like Rotary, Kiwanis, Lions, and so on, and fraternities like the Elks, the Moose, the Eagles, and others. They can solicit members, and they show no ill effects from it!" But, when we look at them, we find breeds apart from Freemasonry.

The former groups are businessmen's clubs, usually holding brief luncheon meetings, having no ritual, and emphasizing direct community service. The latter fraternities are social clubs ("poor men's country clubs," if you will), usually holding many social affairs, having little ritual, and encouraging community service (but not as their major activity). Freemasonry, on the other hand, is a fraternity open to all moral men, usually holding lengthy meetings after work, having an elaborate ritual, and emphasizing individual reformation as the means to community improvement. There are only superficial similarities between these clubs and Freemasonry, so any comparisons are not likely to offer much illumination.

The proper place to look for such comparisons is with an organization that is as much like Freemasonry as possible. It should have at least the following characteristics: a broad base in the community, a female "auxiliary" like the Eastern Star, several collateral branches, something similar to the Shrine for boisterous fun, and "junior branches" for the children. It turns out that the perfect candidate for such an analysis is the Independent Order of Odd Fellows. Both Freemasonry and Odd Fellowship are British imports, though the Odd Fellows are about eighty years younger in the United States, having been started in 1813 in Baltimore. The moral and ethical teachings of the Odd Fellows are so like those of our Craft as to be indistinguishable, and, to an outsider, Odd Fellowship simply seems to be a less elaborate version of Freemasonry.

Each state (with a few minor exceptions) has its own Grand Lodge of Odd Fellows, together with a Grand Encampment of Patriarchs, and a uniformed, military Department of Patriarchs Militant. For the convivial there are the Samaritans, for the ladies there are the Rebekah, and for the boys and girls there are the Junior Lodges and the Theta Rho.

The major organizational difference between Odd Fellows and Freemasons is that the Odd Fellows have a national Sovereign Grand Lodge that controls every branch of the order, except for the Samaritans. Like the Freemasons, the Odd Fellows maintain an impressive number of orphanages and retirement homes, and their charities have done much to relieve the sufferings of mankind. Here then is the only proper organization for comparison with Freemasonry.

In America in 1900, Odd Fellowship had 11,400 lodges and 870,000 members to Freemasonry's 11,700 lodges and 839,000 members. Odd Fellow membership was then 104% of Masonic membership. Around 1915, Freemasonry's membership caught up with that of the Odd Fellows, when both had about 1,500,000 members. Odd Fellowship, however, started losing members in the early 1920s, and the trend accelerated during the Depression. While World War II led to an increase in Masonic membership, the Odd Fellows continued declining, until now they have fewer than 160,000 members in the United States, an 82% decline from 1900! (By contrast, Craft membership today is more than 390% of its membership in 1900.) [8] No study of Masonic membership trends can be considered complete without analyzing this virtual demise of the Odd Fellows.

One of the important explanations for these figures is the membership base of the two groups. John H. White, Grand Sire of the Odd Fellows in 1888, said that American Odd Fellowship is composed "of the great middle, industrial classes almost exclusively; Masonry [is composed] of all grades of society, from the titled and wealthy of this and foreign lands, to the humblest laborer...."[10] This partially explains why the Depression, with its crushing effects on the working class, had much harsher results for Odd Fellowship, but it does not explain enough.

Odd Fellows can solicit members for their lodges, and certainly we must assume that they used this and every possible means to prevent their decline. Following the arguments presented for soliciting Masonic candidates, the Odd Fellows, by their solicitation, should have found men more concerned with their Order and more dedicated to service and attendance; they should have weeded out the lukewarm and strengthened their organization's basic structures. After the Depression and the War passed, if indeed solicitation were the panacea it is claimed to be, our proponents should have expected a spurt of growth in Odd Fellowship, until today it should have been a healthy, thriving, and prosperous organization. The facts, however, stand in stark contrast to the expectations. Unless we can explain why solicitation did not save the Odd Fellows, we cannot begin to hope it win work for us.

Before we change this time-honored custom of ours, a custom that has served us well enough to produce such Craftsmen as Rudyard Kipling, Omar Bradley, J. C. Penney, Norman Vincent Peale, and Harry S Truman, we should consider if there might, just might, be a few other problems we want to face first. For example, our regulations on dual membership were largely written when we were a small town, rural society with little population mobility. Today, these rules ignore the strong attachment for the "Mother Lodge," and all but encourage a man to become inactive in the Craft once he moves from his hometown. Little real education is to be found in our fundamental units, the lodges; a member must have the perseverance to seek further light himself, or give up the search. Our Grand Lodges encourage and support ritual perfection, but treat education and research as unwanted stepchildren.

By long-standing practice, there is virtually no rewarded activity in the lodge that does not involve either presiding or ritual. Further, our consuming concern with the appearance of propriety has led to a Puritanical stuffiness in our affairs. Nearly one hundred years ago, Brother Rob Morris, Poet Laureate of Freemasonry said, "The Order with us has too much of the pulpit, and too little of the table. A due intermixture of both was what the Craft in olden time regarded."[7] Knowing all this, we still wonder why our members seek involvement in the collateral bodies.

It is possible for a brother to become Master of his lodge without ever having seen or given any thought to program planning. Our meetings all too often become sad examples of the triumph of procedure over substance. Imagine for a minute a typical lodge meeting where there will be no degree work, only one ballot, and routine business. In 45 minutes, a competent Master may be able to open the lodge, approve the minutes, pay the bills, read the correspondence, ballot on the petition, and close the lodge. A less able Master may take much more than an hour to do this, which is essentially nothing. I realize that all of these are important to the functioning of a lodge, but for the busy man who has worked all day and who has left his family at home to rush to the meeting, there must be a sense of betrayal. With the possible exception of the ballot, nothing of substance was accomplished, and this scenario is repeated countless times throughout our lodges.

American Masonry seems to have trapped itself into several self-destructive practices. Fifty years ago, our fees and dues were significantly higher in relation to salaries than they are now. After our frightening decline during the Depression, we did not want to risk losing any candidates because of their inability to meet the fees, and so they remained fixed. With the deluge of new members after World War II, there was then no need to raise fees and dues, as expanding rosters kept lodge incomes up. We became complacent and believed that a steady flow of new members was normal and would always keep us financially solvent. But, as initiations declined and inflation raged, we found ourselves ever more strapped for money. Now, with an older membership, many of whom are on fixed incomes, we do not raise our dues for fear of losing members nor do we raise fees for fear of losing candidates.

Low fees and dues discourage lodges from splitting, for a large membership is often essential to financial survival. As M.W. Brother Ernest Poynter, Grand Master of Maryland, said at the 1964 Conference of Grand Masters:

> size begets size, so that already overgrown Lodges continue to grow like weeds and, like weeds, the bigness chokes out those members who had sought friendships and Masonic sociability—who had been fired with desire to work on committees or in the chairs, but soon find that there just isn't anything for them to do.[9]

The results are larger, impersonal lodges and the gradual financial paralysis of our Craft. We are like small children whimpering during a thunderstorm: unaware of what is really happening, unsure of what to do, and frightened by the apparent chaos of nature.

American Freemasonry is currently experiencing difficult times (surely not our first, nor our worst, nor our last). We are unable or unwilling to distinguish between the merely procedural and the truly fundamental. Rather than undertake the difficult (and likely painful) task of deciding which of our time-honored, well-loved, and decrepit procedures are discouraging activity in the Craft, too many of our "leaders," blinded by numbers alone, frantically grasp at the first, the most obvious, and certainly the poorest solution: the solicitation of members. The national debt cannot be retired by printing more money, nor can opening the floodgates of solicitation cure our problems.

Grand Master Poynter summed it up:

> There is nothing wrong with Masonry that cannot be quickly cured by forward-looking Masonic leaders who will have the courage to discard ancient, worn out formalities and to institute fresh and modern approaches to the problem of creating an attractive and desirable new image of Masonry for our many Brothers who have grown "passive and complacent" largely as a result of our failure to provide aggressive and progressive leadership.[9]

Freemasonry has undergone many changes during the twentieth century, and will doubtless undergo many more, but if our leaders will indeed lead and not just conserve, if they will look at long-range solutions and not at short-term problems, if they will seriously reflect and not merely react, then these future changes can only strengthen our gentle Craft and guarantee our Light for future generations.

REFERENCES

1. Carr, Harry. *The Freemason at Work.* 6th ed. London: A. Lewis, Ltd., 1981.

2. Grand Lodge of Illinois, A.F.&A.M. *Proceedings.* Springfield: Grand Lodge, 1979.

3. Grand Lodge of Kansas, A.F.&A.M. *Proceedings.* Topeka: Grand Lodge, 1979.

4. Homer. *The Odyssey.* Translated by S. H. Batcher and Andrew Long. New York: Dodd, Meade, 1959.

5. Hunt, Bruce H. *A Masonic Review.* St. Louis: Grand Lodge of Missouri, 1979.

6. Johnson, David O. "Turning the Craft Outwards." *The New Age* 89, no. 11 (Nov. 1981): 14–17.

7. Morris, Rob. *The Poetry of Freemasonry.* Laureate ed. Chicago: Werner, 1895.

8. Morris, S. Brent. "A Fraternal Abstract of the United States: 1900–1980." Manuscript, Columbia, Md., 1981.

9. Poynter, Ernest L. "How May we Overcome the Passive and Complacent Attitude of so Many of the Craft?" Conference of Grand Masters of Masons in North America. *Proceedings.* February, 1964, 70–76. Washington, DC: Conference of Grand Masters, 1964.

10. Ross, Theo. A. *Odd Fellowship: Its History and Manual.* New York: M. W. Hazen, 1888.

11. Smith, Dwight L. *Why This Confusion in the Temple?* Silver Spring, MD: Masonic Service Association of the United States, 1970.
Presented at the Northeast Conference on Masonic Education & Libraries, Newark, Delaware, May 13, 1983

Landmarks and Liabilities
Mackey's Notorious List and Its Impact on Maryland Masonry

> A mushroom may grow ever so tall, on a boundary line or at a corner, but it will never be mistaken for a landmark
>
> —*Albert Pike on Mackey's "Landmarks"*[1]

Freemasonry in Maryland, as in the rest of the world, is changing. This is a continuing process that began in 1717 at the Goose and Gridiron Tavern in London when four lodges made a radical innovation on the body of Masonry and created the office of Grand Master, an office that prior to that date had been only legendary. The additions, corrections, and elaborations to our Craft have come in fits and spurts since then, and we should not be so naïve to think that our Grand Lodge is immune. What are needed to face the challenges of change are an openness of mind and a flexibility of procedures.

Maryland Masonry is fortunate that its leaders have had minds open to the evolving needs of the Craft. They have laid a solid foundation on which the Grand Lodge has set goals, established programs, and disseminated the tenets of our profession. However, there is a grave danger that we are losing our flexibility of procedures that will be necessary for our survival in the twenty-first century.

At the 1989 Semiannual Communication of the Grand Lodge of Maryland, we witnessed the elimination of informed debate on several potentially vital pieces of legislation and the disenfranchisement of the representatives of the subordinate lodges. This disregard for democratic principles was not part of a conspiracy nor planned with malice, but rather it sadly followed from a strict application of Mackey's so-called "Landmarks of Freemasonry." The Grand Lodge of Maryland has never formally adopted these twenty-five platitudes, but they threaten to become liabilities through a rigid interpretation.

---

1   Albert Pike, "The Landmarks of Freemasonry," in *The Little Masonic Library* (Richmond: Macoy Publishing and Masonic Supply, 1946), vol. 1, 66.

Albert Galatin Mackey is one of the best-known American authors on Freemasonry. What is less well known is that his creative genius often over-shadowed his quest for historical accuracy and truth. In 1858, Mackey invented his list and foisted it upon an unsuspecting American Craft. Soon after there was a headlong rush by "scholars" to create lists of landmarks and thus fill in what they perceived as a nagging gap in Masonic tradition. Right behind these creative writers came the Grand Lodges, each trying to outdo the other in adopting the "true" list of fundamental Landmarks of Freemasonry.

These enterprises resulted in nothing less than confusion in the temple. Of the American Grand Lodges, thirteen have adopted no formal list, five rely upon the Old Charges, ten have produced their own lists (ranging from seven to thirty-nine Landmarks), eight use Mackey by custom, and only thirteen have formally adopted his tabulation.[2] The United Grand Lodge of England, the source and origin of all Freemasonry, has never seen fit to adopt any formal enumeration and in particular has never endorsed Mackey's list, and our English brethren seem none the worse for it.

Where in all of this does the Grand Lodge of Maryland stand?—somewhere between using Mackey by custom and by formal adoption. In November 1939, R.W. Harry C. Mueller, Grand Secretary, wrote that "Maryland has included in its Code Mackey's twenty-five Landmarks. By the adoption of this Code we feel that the twenty-five Landmarks in their entirety were adopted also, although there was no specific mention made of this, nor has there been at any time."[3] Thus, the foundation of Masonic Jurisprudence in Maryland has never been formally adopted!

Isn't the simplest solution to formally adopt Mackey's product and to be done with it? That would easily solve the problem of the status of Mackey's landmarks in Maryland, but like most simple-minded solutions, it's more wrong than right. There is a naïve satisfaction in having an absolute list of guiding principles, and a childlike comfort in being able to assert, "These constitute the Landmarks ... in which it is not in the power of any man, or body men, to make the least innovation."[4] However, naïve satisfaction and

---

2   Masonic Service Association, "The Ancient Landmarks of Freemasonry," in *The Little Masonic Library* (Richmond: Macoy Publishing and Masonic Supply, 1946), vol. 1, 95.

3   Masonic Service Association, "The Ancient Landmarks of Freemasonry," 76–77.

4   Grand Lodge of Maryland, *Maryland Manual of Ancient Craft Masonry* (Baltimore: Grand Lodge, A.F.&A.M., 1935,) C.

childlike comfort should not be the guiding forces of Maryland Freemasonry as it prepares to face the rigors of the twenty-first century.

To begin with, Mackey was simply wrong. Some of his so-called "Landmarks" are universally agreed upon, but most are just creatures of his fertile imagination. Albert Pike's scathing denunciation of Mackey's concoction stands as the damning opinion of contemporary scholar, and Pike was not alone in his condemnation. No serious student of Freemasonry has accepted Mackey's 1858 list in its entirety, nor have more than thirteen Grand Lodges.

"So far as known, no Grand Lodge outside the United States has ever adopted any list of landmarks...."[5] Even a partial list of those disagreeing with Mackey provides a *Who's Who* of Masonic scholarship (See Table 1 and Appendix.)

1856, Rob Moms, Past Grand Master, Kentucky

1858, J. W. S. Mitchell, Past Grand Master, Missouri

1885, Robert Freke Gould, Past Master Quatuor Coronati Lodge No. 2076

1888, Albert Pike, Sovereign Grand Commander, Southern Jurisdiction

1910, George Fleming Moore, Sovereign Grand Commander, Southern Jurisdiction

1919, Roscoe Pound, Dean, Faculty of Law in Harvard University

1923, Joseph D. Evans, Past Grand Master, New York

1924, Melvin M. Johnson, Past Grand Master, Massachusetts

1931, E. W. Timberlake, Jr., Past Grand Mater, North Carolina

1961, Henry Wilson Coil, Fellow of the Philalethes Society

1973, Dwight L. Smith, Past Grand Master, Indiana

Table 1. Some Masonic Scholars Disagreeing with Mackey's "Landmarks"

A Landmark should be something so fundamental, so basic to the fabric of Freemasonry, that any deviation merits immediate condemnation. Mackey's creation fails this test rather miserably. There is no reason to analyze

---

5   Henry W. Coil, et al., *Coil's Masonic Encyclopedia* (New York: Macoy Publishing and Masonic Supply, 1961), 360.

each of his landmarks; a few particulars should suffice. For example, the Grand Lodge of North Carolina not only does not recognize the prerogative of a Grand Master to make Masons at sight (Mackey's Landmark 8), but also does not recognize any Mason made by this method, regardless of whether he may belong to a regularly chartered lodge. Yet we still maintain fraternal relations with the Grand Lodge of North Carolina. Several of the regular European Grand Lodges we recognize use a Grand Masonic Word different from Maryland, thus effectively negating the Mackey's first landmark, the modes of recognition.

Freemasonry recently has come under increasingly vicious attacks from narrow-minded religionists. One of the frequent accusations made against our gentle Craft is that we are a "secret society" with all of the vague connotations of unknown evil that charge carries. Maryland has wrestled with this problem and has tried to solve it with our rather awkwardly worded Standing Resolution No. 8, which says in part "that our Order is not a secret one in the sense that everything that goes on in the lodge room may never be revealed; rather it is an Order which has certain secrets which we do not share with the world outside these doors."[6]

This is all fine and good, but Mackey's Twenty-third Landmark states in simple, plain language, "Freemasonry is a secret society." If we adopt Mackey's invention, then we are declaring to the world that we are indeed a secret society (despite our waffling resolutions to the contrary). If we are not a secret society, then Landmark 23 of Mackey is not a Landmark of Maryland.

The Grand Lodge of Maryland presents another paradox on the one hand we acknowledge by custom Mackey's Landmark 14, "the *right* of every Mason to visit and sit in every regular lodge." On the other hand we ignore this clear, absolute right and allow only the *privilege* of visitation. A brother visiting a Maryland lodge may be denied admission if any member of that lodge personally demands it. In fact, Maryland's deviation from this "landmark" has earned us special condemnation in *Mackey's Masonic Jurisprudence* as an offensive example of a "very contracted view of the universality of Freemasonry. ..."[7]

---

6   Grand Lodge of Maryland, *Reports to the Annual Communication* (Baltimore: Grand Lodge, A.F.&A.M., Nov. 17, 1986), 29.

7   Albert G. Mackey, *Mackey's Masonic Jurisprudence,* rev. by R. I. Clegg (Chicago: Masonic History Co., 1927), 141.

At the 1989 Semiannual Communication of the Grand Lodge of Maryland, an amendment to the Constitution was proposed that would have allowed subordinate lodges to conduct normal business in the 1°. The Committee on Masonic Jurisprudence carefully considered the matter, adhered faithfully to Mackey's landmarks, and made the straightforward decision that "the proposed Amendment ... would violate the Landmarks of Freemasonry and Masonic history and tradition."[8]

This inescapable conclusion that the committee reached by following Mackey's authority is logically precise and historically wrong. On May 18, 1842, the Grand Lodge of Maryland "*Resolved,* That all the business of a lodge, except that of conferring the inferior degrees, and the instruction therein, should be transacted in a Master Mason's Lodge."[9]

In other words, from 1749 to 1842, every lodge in Maryland conducted its business on the 1°—in violation of Mackey's landmarks and Masonic history and tradition! How is it possible that our first ninety-three years of Masonic activity violated the Landmarks of Freemasonry and Masonic history and tradition? For that matter, what does this say about the United Grand Lodge of England, whose lodges have never stopped meeting on the 1°? These contradictions are possible only if Mackey's inventive list is given official status in Maryland, and we abandon our original history and customs.

Finally, there is the example of the recently aborted attempt to provide checks and balances upon the powers of the Grand Master of Maryland. The argument that prevented the amendments from even being discussed was that Mackey's so-called landmarks do not allow the Grand Lodge to limit the authority of the Grand Master. Mackey states with his usual authoritative tone that Grand Masters and Grand Lodges are "coeval" (a highfalutin word that means "of equal antiquity"). However, there is no foundation in fact—only in modern Masonic ritual—that Grand Lodges or Grand Masters existed before that historic 1717 meeting in London.

These lofty, theoretical arguments overlook a fundamental problem: if the Grand Lodge cannot limit the powers of the Grand Master, how did we get the limitations we now have? Perhaps the Grand Architect Himself or-

---

8   Grand Lodge of Maryland, *Reports to the Semi-Annual Communication* (Baltimore: Grand Lodge, A.F.&A.M., May 15, 1989), 29.

9   Edward T. Schultz, *History of Freemasonry in Maryland* (Baltimore: J. H. Mediary, 1887), vol. 3, 67.

dained the requirement that the Grand Lodge has to approve edicts of the Grand Master for them to remain in force? The powers of the Grand Master spring from the consent of the lodges he governs, and they can modify his powers whenever or however they see fit.

The fact is, Mackey's fabrication never has been adopted formally by the Grand Lodge of Maryland nor has it made any particular contribution to our jurisprudence. What is true is that the Grand Lodge of Maryland has regularly ignored Mackey when convenient, though his invention most recently prevented a democratic discussion of important issues facing the Grand Lodge of Maryland. The solution to the confusion is straightforward: drop Mackey's lame "landmarks" (either by agreement or by formal edict or by resolution) and give the Grand Lodge of Maryland the flexibility and authority it needs to face the problems of the future.

APPENDIX

Quotations from Some Masonic Scholars Disagreeing
with Mackey's "Landmarks"

Robert Freke Gould

We shall vainly search in the records of those early times for a full specification of the twenty-five "Landmarks" which modern research pronounces to be both ancient and unalterable. … Of the Ancient Landmarks it has been observed, with more or less foundation in truth: "Nobody knows what they comprise or omit; they are of no earthly authority, because everything is a landmark when an opponent desires to silence you, but nothing is a landmark that stands in his own way."

The History of Freemasonry, New York: John C. Yorston, 1885, vol. 2, 59.

Albert Pike

There is no common agreement in regard to what are and what are not landmarks. That has never been definitely settled. Each writer makes out for himself the list or catalogue of them, according to his own fancy, some counting more of them and others less.

Most of these so-called landmarks were not known either to Ancient Craft Masonry in England or Scotland before the revolution of 1723, or to the new Masonry, as landmarks, for years afterwards. It is a pity that Masonry has not a Pope, or cannot make one of some Grand Master, Editor, or Chairman of a Committee on Foreign Correspondence, endowed with infallibility, to determine the age which a landmark must have to entitle it to call itself a landmark; what is the essential nature of a landmark; how many of the supposed twenty-five are landmarks, and what others the oracular wisdom of the author [Mackey] of this catalogue has overlooked.

Proceedings of the Masonic Veterans Association of Iowa, 1888 (reprinted in *Coil's Masonic Encyclopedia,* New York: Macoy Publishing & Masonic Supply, 1961, 367–59).

E. W. Timberlake Jr.

A number of Grand Lodges have undertaken, by express enactment, to fix what the landmarks shall be within their respective jurisdictions, and these differ very widely. For example, nine American Grand Lodges declare that the ancient charges contain the landmarks, while several Grand Lodges have adopted statements of their own, varying all the way from seven in West Virginia and ten in New Jersey to thirty-nine in Nevada and fifty- four in Kentucky. It would seem obvious, therefore, that, since even a Grand Lodge can neither create nor abolish a landmark, such declaratory enactments cannot be viewed in any other light than as Masonic legislation. ... It is generally conceded that Dr. Mackey's list includes all of the landmarks, but it is not conceded that all those which he enumerates as landmarks, are in reality such.

"The Landmarks of Masonry," *Nocalore* 1 (1931): part 1, 4–16.

Roscoe Pound

The skeptic says, first, that down to the appearance of *Mackey's Masonic Jurisprudence* "landmark" was a term floating about in Masonic writing without any definite meaning. It had come down from the operative Craft where it had meant trade secrets, and had been used loosely for "traditions" or for "authorized ritual" or for "significant historical occurrences," and Oliver had even talked of "obsolete landmarks." Second, he says, the definition of a landmark, the criteria of a landmark, and the fixed landmarks generally received in England and American from 1860 on, come from Mackey. Bro.

Hextall says: "It was more because Mackey's list purported to fill an obvious gap than from any signal claims it possessed that it obtained a rapid circulation and found a ready acceptance." Perhaps this is too strong. But it must be admitted that dogmatism with respect to the landmarks cannot be found anywhere in Masonic writings prior to Mackey and that our present views have very largely been formed—even if not wholly formed—by the influence of his writings....

In reading [Mackey's definition of a landmark] we must bear in mind that it was written in 1856, before the rise of modern Masonic history and before the rise of modern ideas in legal science in the United States. Hence it is influenced by certain uncritical ideas of Masonic history and by some ideas as to the making of customary law reminiscent of Hale's *History of the Common Law*, to which some lawyer may have directly or indirectly referred him. But we may reject these incidental points and the essential theory will remain unaffected—the theory of a body of immemorial recognized fundamentals which give to the Masonic order, if one may say so, its Masonic character, and may not be altered without taking away that character. It is true Mackey's list of landmarks goes beyond this. But it goes beyond his definition as he puts it; and the reason is to be found in his failure to distinguish between the landmarks and the common law.

Lectures on Masonic Jurisprudence, New York: Board of General Activities [Grand Lodge, F. & A.M.], 1941, 32–34.

Henry Wilson Coil

The way to define a thing or a principle is to examine it closely, list its peculiarities, state how it looks and acts, what it does and does not do, and what it is not as well as what it is. Again, the landmarkers reversed the process by attempting to define the unknown thing arbitrarily and, then armed with that prejudicial formula, search through the rituals, the regulations, and even unofficial literature in search of items which would satisfy the definitions. They did not know that the definition is the conclusion, not the beginning of such enquiry. But, worse yet, they commonly included some items which did not conform to their definitions. Of this class, one of the leaders, Mackey, was a striking example. What he called ancient and unwritten principles were in several of his proposals no more than legislation of the premier Grand Lodge set forth in the Constitutions and General Regulations published in 1723. Some that he called universal were not followed in all, possibly not even in a majority of Masonic jurisdiction. Those called unalterable had already been altered in some instances, and Mackey, himself, gave out several additions which altered his unalterable list of twenty-five.

Coil's Masonic Encyclopedia, New York: Macoy Publishing & Masonic Supply, 1961, 364.

Dwight L. Smith

The Grand Lodge of England, which should know a thing or two about the ancient landmarks, never has "adopted" landmarks or in any way attempted to define them other than to make casual references to certain practices. To my knowledge, no Grand Lodge of Freemasons outside the United States has ever become concerned about what the landmarks are, or how many there may be.

Not so in the US. Beginning about the middle of the nineteenth Century, Grand Lodges started trying to define the landmarks and enumerating them. They literally ran races to see how many ancient landmarks they could "adopt" officially. Some lists became so long and so all-inclusive that it was hardly safe to take aim at the brass cuspidor for fear an ancient landmark would be removed. And the hilarious feature about the various lists of "official" and "unalterable" landmarks is that so many are in total disagreement with their neighbors' lists!

"Of Landmarks and Cuspidors," *The Philalethes* 26, no. 1 (Feb. 1973): 6, 22.

References

Coil, Henry W. et al. *Coil's Masonic Encyclopedia.* New York: Macoy Publishing Aid Masonic Supply, 1961.

Gould, Robert Freke et al. *The History of Freemasonry.* New York: John C. Yorston, 1885.

Mackey, Albert G. *Mackey's Masonic Jurisprudence.* Revised by R. I. Clegg. Chicago; Masonic History Co., 1927.

Maryland, Grand Lodge of. *Maryland Manual of Ancient Craft Masonry.* Baltimore: Grand Lodge, A.F.&A.M., 1935.

————. Reports to the Annual Communication. Baltimore: Grand Lodge, A.F.&A.M., Nov. 17, 1986.

————. Reports to the Semiannual Communication. Baltimore: Grand Lodge, A.F.&A.M., May 15, 1989.

Masonic Service Association. "The Ancient Landmarks of Freemasonry." *The Little Masonic Library.* 5 vols. Richmond: Macoy Publishing and Masonic Supply, 1946.

Pike, Albert. "The Landmarks of Freemasonry." *The Little Masonic Library.* 5 vols. Richmond: Macoy Publishing and Masonic Supply, 1946.

Pound, Roscoe. *Lectures on Masonic Jurisprudence.* New York: Board of General Purposes, [Grand Lodge, F.&A.M.], 1941.

Schultz, Edward T. *History of Freemasonry in Maryland.* 4 vols. Baltimore: J. H. Mediary, 1887.

Smith, Dwight L. "Of Landmarks and Cuspidors." *The Philalethes* 26, no. 1 (Feb. 1973).

Timberlake Jr., E. W. "The Landmarks of Masonry." *Nocalore* 1 (1931): part 1.

First published: *The Philalethes Magazine* 44, no. 3 (June 1991)

Table Lodges
A Presentation for the Feast of Tishri in Baltimore

Freemasonry, from its earliest days, has been not only a speculative society, but also a convivial one. One of the early attractions of Masonic membership was the opportunity for the brethren to meet together at social occasions and at festive banquets. American Masonry seems to have lost sight of this vital, ancient tradition, though within the past few decades there has been a resurgence of interest in "Table Lodges."

In the early days of Freemasonry, lodges met in taverns, largely because these were the only buildings in a community that could hold a sizable meeting. However, we must not discount the importance of the easy availability of food and drink—especially drink! Another long-standing Masonic custom, largely lost in America, is the Masonic toast. Special heavy-bottomed glasses were used for the ceremony. After the toast was made and the drink downed, the glasses were slammed down on the tables by the brethren, thus "firing the cannons." This custom still exists in a modified form in England today as the "good fire" given after toasts.

The importance of toasts and drinking to early Maryland lodges is well illustrated by a brief quote from the minutes of the Leonardtown Lodge. The records of the "Lodge—Held at Leonardtown, St. Mary's County," are the oldest lodge records in the United States, except for those of St. John's Lodge in Boston. On November 4, 1761, at the ninth recorded meeting of the lodge, it was "ordered that Brother Fisher get the following articles provided, as soon as possible at the expense of the lodge: A Balloting Box with Ballots; 2 dozen Aprons; 4 dozen Masons' Glasses...."[2] The custom of toasting was apparently so well known that it was unnecessary to be more specific about the type of glasses other than to say "Masons' Glasses." We might also infer, since twice as many glasses as aprons were ordered, that those Masons did twice as much drinking as lodge work!

When Patmos Lodge, No. 70 of Ellicott's Mills (now Ellicott City) laid the cornerstone of the B&O viaduct over the Fredericktown Turnpike Road on July 4, 1829, a local tavern was the focus of some of the events. According to the report in *The Gazette,* the Masonic fraternity of Ellicott's Mills … formed themselves in procession, accompanied by the Grand Lodge of Maryland, and proceeded from the Lodge Room to the cornerstone.… At Thomas's Tavern they were joined by Captain McNeil on the part of the Board of Engineers, and Caspar W. Weaver, Esq., Superintendent of construction.… The master having concluded [the ceremonies], the usual invocation was made, and the corn, wine and oil poured upon the granite.… The Masonic fraternity with their invited guests … then adjourned to Thomas's Hotel.… [1]

Certainly this is far different from Masonic processions of today—our brethren at Patmos Lodge stopped at Thomas's on the way to the ceremonies, and then adjourned to the Tavern after the events!

A Table Lodge is simply a lodge meeting held at a banquet table. Certainly the ceremonies of two centuries ago were simpler, but Masonic ritual was then in a state of flux, changing from lodge to lodge, or even in the same lodge from meeting to meeting. The Table Lodge ceremonies seen today in the United States seem to be derived from the ceremonies of the French in the middle 1700s. This particularly includes the semi-military ceremonies of toasting (for example, calling glasses "cannons" and the drink "powder").

One of our earliest records of a meeting specifically called a "Table Lodge" (as opposed to a meeting held at a banquet table because of convenience) is from Baron Tschoudy in his book *The Blazing Star* (*L'Etoile Flamboyante*). He records a speech given on St. John's day in Winter, 1764, for a Table Lodge (pour une Loge de Table).[3] From this record, we can see that by 1764, the simple tavern meeting had already evolved into a formal banquet with songs, toasts, and elaborate rituals.

The form of a Table Lodge or of a Masonic banquet, such as the Feast of Tishri, however, is not as important as its spirit. As American Masons today discover that there is much more to our Gentle Craft than the recent innovations of ritual memorization, we are drawn to our earlier, discarded heritage. A Masonic banquet is a feast of the spirit as well as of the body. It should be classed with the other great ceremonial meals of our society: Thanksgiving dinner, the Holy Eucharist, Passover Seder. It is an opportunity for brothers to sit at a common table, to break bread together, and to share of themselves. It is in settings such as this that Freemasonry had its starts, and will find renewed strength for the future.

REFERENCES

1. Historic Ellicott City, Inc. *Heritage* 3, no. 2 (July 1976).

2. Schultz, Edward T. *History of Freemasonry in Maryland.* 4 vols. Baltimore: J. H. Mediary, 1884.

3. Tschoudy, Baron Louis Theodore. *L'Etoile Flamboyante, ou la Société des Francs Maçons Considérée sous tous les Aspects,* 1766. 2 vols. Reprint. Paris: Gutenberg Reprints, 1979.

Presented to Albert Pike Lodge of Perfection,
Baltimore, Maryland, September 11, 1985

Maundy Thursday

A Presentation Given in Duluth at the Solemn Feast

It is a special privilege to be in the Valley of Duluth to share Maundy Thursday with you, my fellow Knights Rose Croix. Few Scottish Rite activities are as laden with symbolic meaning as Maundy Thursday, and none celebrate a simpler or more profound concept. This evening we are assembled together to reaffirm our belief in a tenet central to Masonry— the only concept that is worthy of being called a Scottish Rite dogma—a doctrine that has frightened the unenlightened and bigoted for centuries. It is neatly summed up in the simple mandate we commemorate tonight: Love one another.

The idea of proper conduct towards others has been an issue in all civilizations. The ancient Greeks, for example, had a strict code of obligations for hosts towards guests, and many of the classic Greek tragedies centered around the breaking of this code and the punishment brought upon its violators. A neat summary of the Greek model of ethics is attributed to Aristotle: "We should behave to friends as we would wish friends to behave to us."

Now, this is a terrific start down the road to civilized behavior, but it is limited in many ways. First and foremost, the obligation established is only between friends. Guided by Aristotle's rule, it would be entirely acceptable to cheat or swindle or rob or murder those not lucky enough to be our friends. Now, this is better than a world in which there are no friends, and might alone rules, but it is offensive to our concept of Masonic responsibilities.

The Jews, in their continuing quest to understand the laws of God and to fulfill His commandments, produced scholars whose genius continues to shine through the millennia. The Talmud represents the pinnacle of Jewish achievement in social, moral, and ethical guidelines, and it speaks as clearly to us today as it did when completed nearly 2000 years ago. It is a collection of hundreds upon hundreds of volumes of commentaries on and studies of the law and teachings of the Torah.

It provides answers for questions what weren't even imagined by its authors. For example: If you take children to the movies, can you lie about their ages to buy the less expensive children's tickets, especially if you know that all of the other adults are doing the same?

The Talmud's answer from the Torah is a simple "NO." Regardless of what others may do, lying in front of children may encourage them to lie when they are grown, and so is not allowed. However, there are exceptions to every rule. You are permitted to tell an ugly bride that she is beautiful, if this will help make her wedding day happy.

Among the brilliant minds that have labored on the Talmud, Rabbi Hillel deserves a special place of honor. He was born in Babylon about 50 BCE, during the reign of King Herod. Hillel traveled to Jerusalem as a young man to study with the leading Biblical scholars of the day. According to legend, he didn't have enough money to pay his tuition, and so resorted to climbing on the roof of the school to listen to the lectures given in the central court of the building. One day it began snowing in Jerusalem, and Hillel was so absorbed in the lecture that he didn't notice the snow and almost froze to death.

While a member of the strict Pharisee sect, Hillel had a wonderful sense of social justice and concern for his fellow man. My favorite story about the Rabbi shows how his teachings anticipated Jesus's teachings. The time of the story is during his later career when he had become recognized as the foremost Biblical scholar and had established his own school in Jerusalem, known as the Hillel House, to work on the Talmud.

One day, a heathen came and knocked at the door of the Hillel House. A servant answered the door and asked what he wanted with the Rabbi. The heathen replied that he was prepared to be converted to Judaism, but only if Rabbi Hillel could teach him the Torah while the heathen stood on one foot. The servant angrily told the man that he insulted the Rabbi in even thinking that the centuries of Jewish law and tradition could be communicated like that. He was told to leave and not to return with impudent questions. Before the servant could slam the door, Rabbi Hillel appeared and said that he would be happy to fulfill the request. The Rabbi then said, "What is hateful to thyself, do not unto thy neighbor. That is the whole of the Torah, all the rest is commentary." This brief but deep lesson of Rabbi Hillel taken from the book of Tobit is remembered today in Israel's Knesset with a statue of Rabbi Hillel and the heathen.

This deceptively simple advice could provide the foundation for a world where peace, harmony, and happiness reign, if only we weak mortals would follow it. The difficulty with implementing this rule is that so many of us believe that some of our neighbors really deserve horrid treatment, and some of our fellow creatures are such scoundrels that firm punishment is called for— just to teach them a lesson. We and our family and friends, of course, can be given the benefit of the doubt.

Another problem with Rabbi Hillel's advice is that it doesn't tell our neighbors how to act, but rather us. It doesn't tell our neighbors to turn down their stereos late at night or keep their parties quite, only us. Our neighbors are free to behave as they like, giving and expecting according to whatever moral rules they think appropriate. We on the other hand are called to the Rabbi's higher standard: we are to do nothing hateful to our neighbors, regardless of what they may do to us. Consider the attacks on Freemasonry by our critics, such as televangelist John Ankerberg or author Stephen Knight. Our natural reaction to vile attacks like these is to attack back and issue formal rebuttals to these baseless charges, but our ritual admonishes us to be silent, and in fact to do even more: to love our enemies.

We must always be fair, polite, and patient, because anything less would be offensive to us. This is an incredibly tough standard achieve. Like searching for the lost Master's word, we could spend a lifetime striving to attain this goal.

Freemasonry points its members to high ethical standards, just as Rabbi Hillel pointed the heathen to the teachings of the Torah. Our gentle Craft expects us to be good men and true and neither stupid atheists nor irreligious libertines. We are required to obey the moral law and to be peaceable citizens in the state. Further, we are expected to go on foot and out of our way to aid a distressed brother. We are taught to remember a brother's welfare in our daily supplications to God, and to keep his secrets as our own. We have a duty to assist and save a falling brother; and to remind him in a friendly manner of his errors and to aid him in a reformation.

And as if we don't have enough moral instructions and ethical duties and Masonic obligations to fulfill, we Knights Rose Croix are called to follow yet another law. A simple, brief, concise rule of behavior that should guide us in all our actions toward mankind. Some 2000 years ago, Jesus of Nazareth carried Rabbi Hillel's summary of the Torah to its logical conclusion. As He ate with his friends for the last time, He told them in his farewell, "A new commandment I give unto you, Love one another."

Our reaction is to dismiss Jesus's new law of love as impractical, if not impossible to obey literally. The dedicated Masonic student and true Knight Rose Croix should react differently. We should try to learn to subdue our passions, to control our impulses, and to probe our anger so that a personal transformation will begin. Just as the search for the lost Master's word is endless, so too is our attempt to obey the new law.

Let me share with you one of my favorite poems dealing with love of fellow man, "Abou Ben Adhem and the Angel" by Leigh Hunt.

Abou Ben Adhem and the Angel
Leigh Hunt

> ABOU BEN ADHEM (may his tribe increase!)
> Awoke one night from a deep dream of peace,
> And saw, within the moonlight in his room,
> Making it rich, and like a lily in bloom,
> An angel writing in a book of gold:—
> Exceeding peace had made Ben Adhem bold,
> And to the presence in the room he said,
> "What writest thou?"—The Vision rais'd its head,
> And with a look made of all sweet accord,
> Answer'd, "The names of those who love the Lord."
> "And is mine one?" said Abou. "Nay, not so,"
> Replied the Angel. Abou spoke more low,
> But cheerily still; and said, "I pray thee, then,
> Write me as one that loves his fellow-men."
>
> The Angel wrote, and vanish'd. The next night
> It came again with a great wakening light,
> And show'd the names whom love of God had bless'd,
> And lo! Ben Adhem's name led all the rest.

Jesus reached into the hearts of his followers, challenged their basic values, and set them on a lifelong quest for God's Kingdom. Masonry takes men, just one man at a time, and strives to make them better men—not better than their brethren, but better than themselves. Could each of us begin now to rededicate ourselves to the great work of Knights Rose Croix to love one another? Perhaps we can think of an estranged friend, or a business competitor, or a neighbor with whom we have had problems, and try to reconcile our differences, and really try to love them, to offer them help, to show them respect, and to begin to change them through transforming ourselves.

Jesus meant that love should have no limitations. This simple rule is central to the teachings of the Rose Croix degree, and it compels us to a standard of behavior that is almost beyond human achievement. This is the new mandate that we celebrate each year at the Mystical Feast of Knights Rose Croix. We are to love others without any regard for what they may or may not do. We are not to worry about how they may treat or mistreat us; we are simply to love them, expecting nothing in return. We are to love with no strings attached. No obligation is placed on the behavior of others, just on us, and that obligation requires us to ignore our instinctive human urges to be petty and vengeful and deceitful and indifferent, and to strive for the nearly impossible goals of loving without judgment, of loving without expectation of gain, and of loving those who seem unlovable. If we set this simple command as our goal and diligently pursue our quest, then we will indeed be worthy of the title of Knight Rose Croix.

––––––––––––––––––––––––––––

Presented to A.T.C. Pierson Chapter of Rose Croix,
Duluth, Minnesota, April 12, 1990

Leadership Means More than "Faithful Service"

A Perspective on Young Masonic Leaders

You must seriously wonder if many of the men who have been Grand Master really wanted to SERVE the Grand Lodge, or just live long enough to become a Past Grand Master.[1]

—John E. Kelly, P.G.M.

I t is unusual today to see young Masons in their twenties and thirties with responsible fraternal leadership positions, and this state of affairs is a recent innovation.

Before he was thirty, Thomas Smith Webb was a giant in the development of American Masonic ritual. His itinerant lecturing and his *The Freemason's Monitor; or Illustrations of Freemasonry* formed the ritualistic foundation upon which nearly all of our Grand Lodges have built their work. He published this classic volume in 1797 at twenty-six, the same year he helped organize the General Grand Chapter of Royal Arch Masons for the Northern States of American and was elected its first General Grand Scribe.

When Webb died in 1819, Jeremy Ladd Cross, thirty-six, succeeded him as the nation's leading Masonic lecturer and published his famous book, *The True Masonic Chart or Hieroglyphic Monitor,* the first illustrated Masonic monitor. Its artwork has influenced virtually every American monitor since.

Webb and Cross are but two of many examples of brethren whose recognition was on the basis of something other than time in grade. They were leaders selected for their merit, not their seniority.

The Craft, however, has long had an ambivalent attitude towards selecting its leaders. In our fraternity's first published regulations, Anderson's 1723 *Constitutions of the Freemasons,* we read under the fourth "general head:"

---

1 John E. Kelly, "The Grand Lodge of Texas: A Management Review," William M. Taylor Chapter, The Philalethes Society, August 20, 1988, 2.

IV. *Of* MASTERS *WARDENS* Fellows, *and Apprentices.*

All Preferment among *Maſons* is grounded upon real Worth and perſonal Merit only; ... Therefore no *Maſter* or *Warden* is choſen by Seniority, but for his Merit.[2]

However in 1738 when Anderson published an expanded edition of the *Constitutions* with his notorious "traditional" history, we see the real value our early brethren placed on merit over seniority. Prior to the historic meeting on St. John the Baptist's Day in 1717 that created the premier Grand Lodge, brethren from the four old lodges "met at the said Apple-Tree [Tavern], and having put into the Chair the oldest Master Mason (now the Master of a Lodge), they constituted themselves a Grand Lodge pro Tempore in Due Form."[3]

For this radical band, so intent on altering the body of Masonry as it then existed, seniority was more important than merit. Now, it may have been that letting the oldest Past Master assume the Grand East was just an expedient rule of order, and that seniority was no worse (but certainly no better) then drawing straws. However, we can only judge from the limited records available, and they seem to speak rather clearly for themselves.

How then has the modern Masonic fraternity followed this balancing of merit and seniority? The answer is fairly obvious to anyone who has endured Masonic "elections" just a few times. The notion that a Warden, no matter how well qualified, could be elected on merit without going through the line is farfetched, except in those lodges so desperate for warm bodies to fill their chairs that anyone will do. As Sovereign Grand Commander Francis G. Paul, 33° observed in his 1988 allocution, "we are less concerned with merit and performance than we are with faithfulness."[4]

The Scottish Rite Northern Jurisdiction has been blessed with many great leaders, and in any list of them John James Joseph Gourgas must rank prominently. In 1813, Emanuel De La Motta from the Charleston Supreme Council traveled to New York to settle the legitimacy of the irregularly or-

---

2   Lionel Vibert, "Anderson's Constitutions of 1723," in *The Little Masonic Library*, 5 vols. (Richmond: Macoy Publishing and Masonic Supply, 1946), vol. 1, 234.

3   Lewis Edwards and W. J. Hughan, *Anderson's Constitutions of 1738* (Bloomington, IL: Masonic Book Club. 1978), 109.

4   Francis G. Paul "A Beacon for the 21st Century," *The Northern Light* 19, no. 4 (Nov. 1988): 7.

ganized Cerneau and Bideaud Supreme Councils. He regularized the Bideaud group and crowned Gourgas an Inspector General. The next day, at the tender age of thirty-six, Gourgas was elected Grand Secretary General.

Giles Fonda Yates helped Gourgas in his struggles to keep the Northern Supreme Council together. Yates, twenty-six, and others revived the Lodge of Perfection at Albany in 1822, and the next year he became its Master. In 1824 he established four other Lodges of Perfection in New York, and one year later he received the 33° and became an active member of the Southern Supreme Council. Yates began to exert his efforts for the Northern Supreme Council when he was elected Lieutenant Grand Commander at thirty-six, and he was rewarded not for his faithfulness but for his merit.

The penchant today for rewarding faithful, plodding service produces faithful, plodding officers—men who have had their enthusiasm drained from them by the numbing path to the East. And those who do remain on the path for their brief, shining moment in the Grand East seem to be driven by little more than enthusiasm. Our grand officers are too often eager boosters with scant time for more than platitudes. Travel schedules alone limit their ranks to the retired or the wealthy or those with few civic, professional, or religious commitments.

In all too many grand bodies, the committees (and the real machinery) are run by a small handful of brethren who treat their positions as sinecures. They are usually benign dictators, zealously working for their vision of what is best for Masonry, but they are dictatorial nonetheless. This limited turnover of leadership is a hallmark of an aging organization. In his book, *Oligarchy in Fraternal Organizations*, Alvin J. Schmidt observed that "fraternal organizations have significantly higher rates of leadership turnover during their first ten years of existence than they have during their most recent decade."[5]

It would be foolish to argue that experience is not crucial to a leader, especially in an organization that values tradition as highly as we do, but more than mere endurance is needed to lead Freemasonry into the twenty-first century. The most obvious problem with equating long, faithful service with leadership qualities is organizational constipation, due to the misguided notion that if one just waits long enough (and doesn't rock the boat

---

5   Alvin J. Schmidt, *Oligarchy in Fraternal Organizations* (Detroit: Gale Research, 1973), 56.

in the process), he can have his "turn." A less obvious but potentially more damaging problem is the disenchantment of young Masons.

All evidence indicates that for at least the last forty years, the average age at initiation has been in the early thirties.[6] If the common model of Masonic activity is followed, then these initiates will arrive in the Easts of their lodges before they are forty—still quite young by Masonic standards. And what can these eager (if their spirits haven't been sapped by mindlessly going through the line) leaders expect for their years of effort? Most likely, an organization that is dominated by the faithfully persistent who insist on conformity as the way to eventual recognition and reward.

Well, why should we think that youth is any better an indicator of ability than lengthy service? We shouldn't, but then again we shouldn't venerate a system that encourages a succession of loyal brethren to enjoy their "fifteen minutes of fame" for little better reason than patience. As Commander Paul has said, "We should be reaching for the best, the most qualified—those who have the ability to move our fraternity forward."[7]

Perhaps it is worth reviewing the activities of a few more of our earlier brethren who advanced on the basis of their abilities, not their age. New York saw the election of DeWitt Clinton as Grand Master in 1806 when he was thirty-seven. At forty-five he was Grand Master of the Grand Encampment of Knights Templar, and at forty-seven he became the General Grand High Priest. Rob Morris was Grand Master of Kentucky in 1857 when he was thirty, and two years later he conceived and arranged the degrees of the Order of the Eastern Star.

In 1842, the Grand Lodge of South Carolina elected its most famous Grand Secretary, Albert Gallatin Mackey, thirty-five. He became the Grand Secretary General of the Southern Supreme Council two years later. Mackey recognized the ability of another young (at least by today's standards) Mason, when he conferred the 4° through the 32° upon Albert Pike in 1853. Four years later, after revising all of the Scottish Rite degrees, Pike received the

---

6   R. Lee Lockwood, "Be Ye Doers of the Word, and not Hearers Only," *Transactions of the Texas Lodge of Research* 10 (1976): 240–41; Masonic Service Association, *Ages of Initiates* (Washington: The Masonic Service Association, 1940), 2; and Ralph E. Whipple, "Ages and Occupations of 1968 Iowa Initiates," *Grand Lodge Bulletin [Grand Lodge of Iowa]* 70, no. 4 (April 1969): 106.

7   Paul "A Beacon for the 21st Century," 7.

33° and the next year became an Active Member of the Southern Supreme Council. In 1859 Pike, fifty, was elected Sovereign Grand Commander.

Starting with the formation of the General Grand Chapter in 1797, it's clear that young men have made the most exciting, original, and lasting innovations upon the body of Masonry. In the nineteenth century, men were involved in all civic and religious activities at younger ages than today, and perhaps naturally expected the same opportunities from Masonry. If organizing and expanding the Craft didn't provide enough active involvement, then a disaffected young Mason could always start his own group.

The Shrine was started in 1871 by two young Masons, Walter M. Fleming and William J. Florence, thirty-three and forty, respectively. Fleming went on to become Potentate of Mecca Temple the next year, when he also received his 33°, and was Imperial Potentate at thirty-eight. The Scottish Rite can count among its founders in 1801 several youngsters: Frederick Dalcho, thirty-one; Comte de Grasse-Tilly, thirty-six; Emanuel De La Motta, forty; James Moultrie, thirty-five; and Isaac Auld, thirty-two.

Robert Wentworth Little created almost from scratch two of our most exclusive organizations, and then convinced the Masonic establishment that membership in them should be highly prized. Little, twenty-six, invented the Order of the Red Cross of Constantine in 1865,[8] and the next year, to top his first coup, he fashioned the Societas Rosicruciana in Anglia (S.R.I.A.) as a Masonic order and became its first Supreme Magus.[9]

These creative impulses have not been confined to nineteenth century Craftsmen. Harold Van Buren Voorhis was thirtyhow-four in 1928 when he became one of the original forty Fellows of the Philalethes Society, and he was thirty-eight when he helped form the Allied Masonic Degrees of the United States and the Grand College of Rites. For all of the prominence that Voorhis later achieved in the various allied bodies, the real title of Great Originator belongs to a much less well known Mason: John Raymond Shute of Monroe, North Carolina.

Shute was only twenty-seven when he invented the Knights of the York Cross of Honor and brought the Holy Royal Arch Knight Templar Priests

---

8   Harold V. B. Voorhis, *The Order of the Red Cross of Constantine* (New York: Press of Henry Emmerson, 1963), 11.

9   Harold V. B. Voorhis, *Masonic Rosicrucian Societies* (New York: Press of Henry Emmerson, 1968), 26–26.

to our shores. The next year, 1932, he imported and organized the Allied Masonic Degrees and created the Grand College of Rites and the Society of Blue Friars. In 1934, he and William Mosley Brown established the Knights Beneficent of the Holy City (Chevaliers Bienfaisants de la Cité Sainte or C.B.C.S.), both having received the degrees earlier in Geneva.

As if these were not enough, in 1936 he imported the Knight Masons of Ireland, which eventually became the Knight Masons of America. This must be something of a record: seven major, thriving Masonic bodies organized by age thirty-two.

Does all of this mean that we should only let Masons under forty lead the Craft, that our only hope rests with the new and excited brother ready to build on the innovations of his illustrious predecessors? Not at all! It only means that we must look beyond men who have "put in the time," and be willing to give real leaders a chance and the time in office to make meaningful contributions. We must begin to change our worship of faithful servants and their defense of the status quo. "But then we Masons are notorious (not famous, for goodness sake!) for trying to maintain the status quo, thinking we are protecting the "body of Masonry." What bunk!"10 Just think what the body of Masonry would be like today without the innovations of its young radicals in the East.

References

Coil, Henry Wilson, et al. *Coil's Masonic Encyclopedia*. New York: Macoy Publishing and Masonic Supply, 1961.

Denslow, William R. *10,000 Famous Freemasons*. 4 vols. Missouri: Missouri Lodge of Research, 1957–1960.

Edwards, Lewis and W. J. Hughan. *Anderson's Constitutions of 1738*. Bloomington, Ill.: Masonic Book Club, 1978.

Kelly, John E. "The Grand Lodge of Texas: A Management Review." William M. Taylor Chapter, The Philalethes Society, August 20, 1988.

---

10 John E. Kelly, "The Grand Lodge of Texas," 15.

Lockwood, R. Lee. "Be Ye Doers of the Word, and not Hearers Only." *Transactions of the Texas Lodge of Research* 10 (1975): 240–41.

Masonic Service Association. *Ages of Initiates.* Washington: The Masonic Service Association, 1940.

Paul, Francis G. "A Beacon for the 21st Century." *The Northern Light* 19, no. 4 (Nov. 1988): 6–7.

Schmidt, Alvin J. *Oligarchy in Fraternal Organizations.* Detroit: Gale Research, 1973.

Vibert, Lionel. "Anderson's Constitutions of 1723." *The Little Masonic Library,* 5 Vols. Richmond: Macoy Publishing and Masonic Supply, 1946.

Voorhis, Harold V. B. *Masonic Rosicrucian Societies.* New York: Press of Henry Emmerson, 1958.

———. *The Order of the Red Cross of Constantine.* New York: Press of Henry Emmerson, 1963.

Whipple, Ralph E. "Ages and Occupations of 1968 Iowa Initiates." *Grand Lodge Bulletin [Grand Lodge of Iowa]* 70, no. 4 (April 1969): 105–6.

First published: *The Northern Light* 20, no. 3 (August, 1989)

A Radical in the East

The Reflections of a High priest on His Year in the East

Loyalty to petrified opinion never yet broke a chain or freed a soul.

—Mark Twain

A s a man matures, his thinking about various things changes. Some of these changes are gradual developments; some are sudden, abrupt turnarounds. 1 would like to share with you a shift in my thinking about Freemasonry of the latter type. My comments deal most specifically with the chapter, though they are applicable to the lodge or any other organization. My thinking was radicalized while I served as High Priest of Zeredathah Chapter No. 35 in Laurel, Maryland. I may not persuade you to my thinking, but at least I hope to make you pause and consider.

My road to becoming a radical began innocently one evening before the opening of chapter. I was concerned with the usual pre-meeting worries: attendance, officers, programs, and time. Especially time, as that evening we had a fair amount of business, and I wanted to close early. I recall thinking to myself: "Open—15 minutes; read and approve the minutes—5 minutes; ballot—10 minutes; announcements—10 minutes; close—10 minutes." Already I saw an hour's work ahead of me, assuming no one became long-winded, and that didn't even include business. Then the Secretary handed me a note with the name of a recently deceased Companion. My first thought was, "Damn! Another three minutes at least for a eulogy and a prayer."

As I thought over the meeting while driving home that evening, I recalled with growing revulsion my reaction to the death of our Companion. His death had not touched me in the least—his passing did not mean to me a loss of fellowship, but only a few minutes longer to spend in chapter. What a perversion of Masonic principles my thinking had become! As I tried to decide what caused me to change so, I realized that my thinking had abruptly shifted.

I recalled our Affirmation Sunday service at a local church where there had been an unpleasant confrontation about whether we should wear our aprons. An older Past High Priest felt that we should follow the Grand Chapter's suggestion and wear our aprons to show the world that we were Royal Arch Masons and proud of it. On the other hand, I maintained that we were at the church to worship, not to impress the congregation. The settlement of this disagreement was that some Companions wore their aprons, some didn't, and I felt smugly self-righteous. That is, until I later reflected on the day. Then I realized that while I had made pious noises about the joy of worshipping together, my real concern had been to wheedle and cajole enough Companions to attend so that the chapter (and especially the High Priest) would not be embarrassed by sparsely filled pews. Was this what our Affirmation Sunday was supposed to be about?

Then my thoughts went to our efforts to gain new members. Were we interested in increasing our circle of friends, sharing our fellowship, or helping a brother find that which was lost? Not on your life! We had much simpler and baser motives. We needed more money, for one thing, and initiation fees were an easy source of income. By increasing our rolls, we would show the world that we were a healthy and vibrant organization; we would reestablish our self-importance (for if we weren't important, why would all of these people seek membership?), and, perhaps most significantly, we would get new officer material. What could be a more urgent task for Masonic officers than to perpetuate themselves?

Kindled by the death of a companion and fueled by some reflection on Capitular Masonry, my old thinking burned away. The time had now come for me to reevaluate my point of view towards the chapter. The fundamental question was: "What is the purpose of Royal Arch Masonry?" My answer was fourfold: preservation, transmission, encouragement, and enhancement. Our chapters are predicated upon preserving the Legend of the Recovery and the philosophy and way of life that is Freemasonry, and transmitting them to our successors.

We also serve to encourage a dynamic interest in our Craft, and to enhance this interest by offering further opportunities for fellowship and service.

If these indeed are our purposes, how do we fulfill them? The ritual serves as our fundamental method for preserving and transmitting the Legend of the Recovery. In our chapter rituals, we elaborate upon and expand the basic tenets of the Craft. Our ceremonies act as a binding force that permits us to enlarge our sense of unity by sharing common experiences. The formality of our procedures, customs, and (at least in Maryland) dress emphasizes the seriousness of our intent; it serves to set us apart from other, more informal groups. And yet, with these lofty purposes and means to achieve them, we fall far, far short of the mark. What has gone wrong?

There is no one simple answer. However, I will share with you what I observe to be some of our more glaring errors. Our formality all too often degenerates into a caricature of the solemnity we hope to attain. Perhaps when evening clothes were a standard item in any gentleman's wardrobe, black tie was an appropriate dress for chapter. Today, when few social functions require black tie and even fewer men own a tuxedo, our formality is out of place. If formal dress is the genuine desire of an individual chapter, then it should be vigorously encouraged. But to put a blanket requirement on all chapters—large and small, city and country—is to invite stagnation and eventual suffocation. The result is, sadly, a cartoon-like scene of ill-fitting tuxedos bought decades ago and kept in service well beyond their natural lives. Presiding over this setting is a High Priest, without his own top hat, who borrows a faded, frayed, and wrong-sized refugee from the coat closet, and then attempts to represent the glory of Solomon!

Ceremony could be the spice of a chapter meeting, but like a spice, it should not overwhelm. If only we followed this maxim! Unfortunately, at least twenty to thirty minutes of each meeting is spent in the tedium of opening and closing. The repetitive nature of these exercises numbs the mind and bores the onlooker. We have all seen ritual bastardizations that produce "short form" ceremonies. These informal alterations indicate a crying need for more fundamental changes, but it is a cry that is seldom heeded. Rather than ask why we persist in using ceremonies created in and ideally suited for the previous century, our Companions slowly drift away, never to return.

When we look at our ritual, we cannot help but be impressed at the position of preeminent importance it has in our affairs. Its importance, I feel, has been bloated entirely out of proportion. Consider for a moment the thousands of man-hours spent on ritual—memorization, rehearsal, exemplification, conferral—and contrast this with the efforts spent on charity or education or even fellowship. It is a rare chapter that does not spend the major part of its time and efforts on ritual, to the exclusion of almost anything else. It is my disturbing observation that ritual has ceased to be a means to an end, the method by which we preserve and transmit our heritage, but rather it has become an end in itself.

While I was in the East, I was advised to hold more rehearsals so we could confer the degrees proficiently. We needed to confer the degrees so we could get new members who were needed to become officers who were needed to attend rehearsals so we could confer the degrees proficiently. We're caught on a treadmill and too few realize it. Our older members long for the halcyon days when weekly rehearsals were packed with eager young Companions longing to be appointed to the line. Those days, if they ever really existed, are past us. It is true that a healthy, strong chapter has excellent degree work, just as it excels in all activities. However, it is folly to think that a crash program in upgrading ritual performance alone will materially improve an ailing chapter.

Having outlined what I consider to be our purposes and some of our failings, I would be remiss if I didn't offer a few suggestions on how we could improve. We could begin by allowing more individuality in our chapters. Some chapters may wish to meet twice a month with a full line of officers in black tie and to confer degrees on demand. Others may want to meet quarterly with only nine Companions in informal dress and to send candidates to other chapters or festivals for their degrees. The current notion of the ideal chapter is one that is large, has a full line of officers, meets frequently, rehearses religiously, and has a waiting list of prospective officers. This ideal at one time may have been common, and for the nineteenth century and even the early twentieth century was perfect, but it is certainly the exception now. We must allow our chapters to find equivalent expressions for their zeal in Capitular Masonry without feeling inadequate. The alternative is to continue as we are, with chapters withering as they become trapped in an endless cycle of failure.

The words *spontaneous* and *lively* are seldom used to describe chapter meetings. Why not encourage a return of activities that not only promote fellowship but also are fun? These could include Table Chapters, dinners, and—as heretical as the suggestion may be—liquor served as refreshments or with a meal. American Freemasonry was bitten at an early age by the temperance bug and has never quite recovered. Capitular Masonry could take a progressive step for the Craft by permitting chapters to serve liquor, and at the same time encourage a less puritanical image of Masonry.

Our opening and closing rituals (not to mention most other routine procedures) should be streamlined. We really don't need ten or more officers in a chapter. Certainly the Veilsmen are unnecessary as is probably the Principal Sojourner. Ideally we should have both a long and short form opening and closing. The latter exist widely in bastard form and need only to be recognized and standardized. I've heard many say that short form ceremonies should never be allowed because the long forms would not be used again. If there is such a willingness to abandon our current forms, perhaps they have outlived their usefulness.

Finally, I'll share with you my most radical thought: Our degrees need to be changed! Masonic ritual as we know it was born in the late seventeenth century. It grew and adapted to serve the Craft as the Craft evolved. It varied locally, and was a living, changing expression of the differing interpretations of our ritual heritage. Then, in the early to mid-nineteenth century, possibly in response to excessive variation and extreme interpretations, our ritual became uniform, rigid, and ossified. It was declared that the interpretations and usages of the middle 1800s would henceforth and forevermore be the orthodox ritual.

As beautiful and meaningful as our ritual may be, I'm not convinced that our 1850 version is any better than a 1750 one, and I'm certainly sorry that I'll never see a 1950 interpretation. Our ritual is indeed impressive, but it should be as we have plagiarized from the finest sources—Shakespeare, the King James Bible, and others. However, great portions are wordy, turgid, anachronistic, unhistorical, and all but impossible to follow. When an evening devoted to the Royal Arch degree alone can drag on to nearly midnight, we cannot help but run off workers as well as sideliners. The task before us is one that will require delicacy and will cause howls of pain, but at the least must be seriously considered.

It is painfully obvious that something is wrong with Capitular Masonry. Our membership is declining, as is that of most fraternal organizations, but more alarming is the fact that the percentage of Craftsmen who join the chapter is also declining. The reasons for this downtrend are neither simple nor clear; otherwise, we would have eliminated them long ago. As conditions continue to deteriorate, many of our Companions take on a siege mentality, perhaps feeling that they are the last guardians of the sanctum sanctorum.

They call, with increasing stridency, for a return to what they perceive as the virtues of our earlier days of strength: rehearsals, degree work, and conformity. To them, any change at all is tantamount to surrender.

On the other hand, I, as a self-confessed radical, want a more imaginative solution. While we still operate from a position of relative stability and strength, we should seek bold innovations. Surely we can preserve and transmit our teachings by some more flexible method. Certainly we can encourage and enhance fellowship and interest in the Craft less stodgily. Novelty will not guarantee success, nor will change be without failure. However, if we must fail, I would rather fail by trying than by acquiescence. When we pass on, as shall all things flesh, I want to go with a bang and not a whimper.

First published: *Royal Arch Mason Magazine* 13, no. 8 (Winter 1980)

Afterword to the First Edition

When my friend Jerry Marsengill telephoned me to ask me to become his assistant I thought for a moment and said yes. (It was always hard for me to say no to Jerry). My expectation was that I would have a long time to "sit at the master's feet" and learn from him.

Unfortunately for all of us, Jerry was taken from us and I was thrust into the role of shepherding this book to publication with no experience or expertise to draw upon. Fortunately for Iowa Research Lodge No. 2, the author of this book is an accomplished editor and were it not for his insistence and effort this would not be the quality production that we want to give to our members.

I want to express my appreciation to Brent Morris for his work and for all that he has taught me. From our first meeting on the evening in July that the floods hit Des Moines (he was in Iowa to give the first annual Jerald E. Marsengill Lecture), I have learned from him. He has been patient with this novice editor and I hope that our association and friendship will continue to grow. I thank him and I also thank Keith Arrington, Tom Dean, and Tom Gruis, my fellow editor/researchers. We all hope that you will enjoy this presentation of Iowa Research Lodge No. 2.

JAY COLE SIMSER

Index

Clausen, Henry C., GC SC SJ, on tightly held intelligence 73
Clinton, DeWitt, GM NY 118
Coil, Henry Wilson on landmarks 102–103
community involvement, reason for joining Freemasonry 19
Constitutions of the Free-Masons, J. Anderson
  1st ed. (1723) 53, 67, 115
  2nd ed. (1738) 80
Crawford, John, GM MD 65
Cross, Jeremy L., Masonic lecturer 115

D

Dalcho, Rev. Frederick, GC SC USA 119
"Death of the Grand Master, The," R. Morris 63–65
De La Motta, Emmanuel 116, 119
Denslow, Ray Vaughn on pioneer Freemasonry and religion 17
Dermott, Laurence, GrSec England (A) 68
Duff, Alexander, GM Manitoba on judging Freemasonry 53
Duluth, MN, SR Bodies 109
Dumfries MS. No. 4 (ca. 1710) 77
Dyer, CAPT Thomas H., USN 71–74

E

Eagles, Fraternal Order of 88
Eastern Star, Order of, membership, 20th century 9–11
  chart 10
  statistics 26
Elements of Geometry, Euclid (ca. 300 BCE) 79
Elks, Benevolent and Protective Order of, membership, 20th century 12–14, 88
  chart 13
  statistics 31
Euclid (fl. 300 BCE) 77

F

F&AM vs. AF&AM 59
Ferguson, Charles W. on benefits of fraternalism 17
First Degree, holding meetings on 99
Fleming, Walter M., Shriners founder 119
Florence, William J., Shriners founder 119
Franklin, Benjamin, GM PA 68
fraternal membership, US *See also* specific groups
  1920 1, 7
  four clusters of groups 7–26
    chart 9

G

gothic constitutions of Freemasonry 77
Gould, Robert Freke on landmarks 100
Gourgas, J. J. J., GrSecGen SC NMJ 116–117
Grand College of Rites 119, 120
Grotto (Mystic Order Veiled Prophets of the Enchanted Realm), last year of growth
     before Depression 3

H

Harris Poll, attitudes towards Shriners 50
Haswell, Nathan B., GM VT 62
Hibernians, Ancient Order of 16
"Hidden Secrets of A Master Mason, The" 75–84
Highland Park Lodge, No. 1150, Dallas, TX 59–66
Hillel, Rabbi 110
Holy Royal Arch Knight Templar Priests 119–122
Howard, Benjamin C., GM MD 62
Hunt, Bruce H., GM MO on solicitation 86
Hunt, Leigh, "Abou Ben Adhem and the Angel" 112

I

INRI 76
insurance, offered by fraternal groups 1

J

Jenkins, Daniel C., GM OH on member demographics 49
Johnson, David O., SGIG OR on solicitation 86, 87
Jolicoeur, Prof. Pamela on SR publication themes 53
Jones, Preston, quoted 7

K

Kansas, GL, 1976 member survey 20
Kelly, John E., GM TX on GM motives to serve 115
Kessler, Burton A. 54
Kiwanis International 3, 50, 88
Knight Masons of America 42, 120
Knight Rose Croix 112, 113
Knights Beneficent of the Holy City 120
Knights of Columbus
  associate & insurance members 21–22
  membership, 20th century 12–14
    chart 13
    Depression, effects of 21–22
    last year of growth before Depression 3

V

W, X

Y

Z

Related Titles from Westphalia Press

A Place in the Lodge: Dr. Rob Morris, Freemasonry and the Order of the Eastern Star
by Nancy Stearns Theiss, PhD

Ridiculed as "petticoat masonry," critics of the Order of the Eastern Star did not deter Rob Morris' goal to establish a Masonic organization that included women as members. Morris carried the ideals of Freemasonry through a despairing time of American history.

Brought to Light: The Mysterious George Washington Masonic Cave
by Jason Williams MD

The George Washington Masonic Cave near Charles Town, West Virginia, contains a signature carving of George Washington dated 1748. This book painstakingly pieces together the chronicled events and real estate archives related to the cavern in order to sort out fact from fiction.

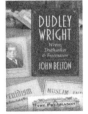

Dudley Wright: Writer, Truthseeker & Freemason
by John Belton

Dudley Wright (1868-1950) was an Englishman and professional journalist who took a universalist approach to the various great Truths of Life. He travelled though many religions in his life and wrote about them all, but was probably most at home with Islam.

History of the Grand Orient of Italy
Emanuela Locci, Editor

No book in Masonic literature upon the history of Italian Freemasonry has been edited in English up to now. This work consists of eight studies, covering a span from the Eighteenth Century to the end of the WWII, tracing through the story, the events and pursuits related to the Grand Orient of Italy.

The Great Transformation: Scottish Freemasonry 1725-1810
by Dr. Mark C. Wallace

This book examines Scottish Freemasonry in its wider British and European contexts between the years 1725 and 1810. The Enlightenment effectively crafted the modern mason and propelled Freemasonry into a new era marked by growing membership and the creation of the Grand Lodge of Scotland.

Getting the Third Degree: Fraternalism, Freemasonry and History
Edited by Guillermo De Los Reyes and Paul Rich

As this engaging collection demonstrates, the doors being opened on the subject range from art history to political science to anthropology, as well as gender studies, sociology and more. The organizations discussed may insist on secrecy, but the research into them belies that.

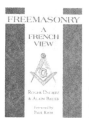

Freemasonry: A French View
by Roger Dachez and Alain Bauer

Perhaps one should speak not of Freemasonry but of Freemasonries in the plural. In each country Masonic historiography has developed uniqueness. Two of the best known French Masonic scholars present their own view of the worldwide evolution and challenging mysteries of the fraternity over the centuries.

Worlds of Print: The Moral Imagination of an Informed Citizenry, 1734 to 1839
by John Slifko

John Slifko argues that freemasonry was representative and played an important role in a larger cultural transformation of literacy and helped articulate the moral imagination of an informed democratic citizenry via fast emerging worlds of print.

Why Thirty-Three?: Searching for Masonic Origins
by S. Brent Morris, PhD

What "high degrees" were in the United States before 1830? What were the activities of the Order of the Royal Secret, the precursor of the Scottish Rite? A complex organization with a lengthy pedigree like Freemasonry has many basic foundational questions waiting to be answered, and that's what this book does: answers questions.

Printed in Great Britain
by Amazon

80127756R00092